YOU CAN'T COME BACK FOR SECONDS

Dolly Kyle in Bull Riding Competition – 1945

Life in the Nevada Frontier

Dolly Kyle

outskirtspress

DENVER, COLORADO

You Can't Come Back for Seconds
Life in the Nevada Frontier
All Rights Reserved.
Copyright © 2012 Dolly Kyle
v2.0

Outskirts Press, Inc.
http://www.outskirtspress.com

ISBN: 978-1-4327-9091-2

Outskirts Press and the "OP" logo are trademarks belonging to Outskirts Press, Inc.

PRINTED IN THE UNITED STATES OF AMERICA

Dedicated to:

My Grandmother

who taught me what it means to love life and live it to the fullest. She told me early on: Dolly, you only get one pass at this world, so make it a good one, because you can't come back for seconds!

And to my eldest child—my beautiful daughter,

Patti Jones Capurro,

born November 20, 1951, and passed October 6, 2010. Patti was a skilled barrel racer;

a highway construction worker, and also an inspector for the USDA (both positions in Kansas); and she also delivered livestock to John Ascuaga's ranch. She worked for Walco Veterinary in Fallon for 22 years. And she ran "Cow Patti's Cafe" at Gallagher's Livestock Auction for awhile.

Table of Contents

Introduction..................................... i

Nevada...1

Back to California............................ 12

My First Husband 16

Nevada Again............................... 21

Husband Number Two.................... 25

A Love Affair................................ 32

A Movie-Star Sighting 36

A Lot of Pancakes 38

Deputy for a Day........................... 45

Clowning Around, Some Drama,
and Santa 48

Husband Number Three 54

Idaho...56

Nevada Calls Me Back 65

Husband Number Four 70

A '70s Woman Unto Herself........................ 72

Husband Number Five................................. 79

Time For a Change ~
Humor Ever the Same................................. 83

Husband Number Six ~
Saving the Best for Last 91

Going Home 114

Introduction

I was born to a 16-year-old, unwed girl with epilepsy. It was October 1928. We lived in Sacramento, California. My Mother suffered through several seizures each day, so, for the first several years of my life, I was virtually raised by my grandparents. My Grandmother was Spanish, and my Grandfather was Italian.

Grandmother was an amazing woman. She worked for the courts in Sacramento as an interpreter; she spoke three languages. One of my earliest and fondest memories of her is the fact that she is the one who donned me with the name Dolly. My birth-given name is Edna, but one day Grandmother and I were out taking a walk. I was proudly wearing my pretty pink jammies that Grandmother had sewn for me and white shoes. A woman passerby exclaimed,

"What a cute little doll you are," and from that day on, Grandmother called me Dolly.

Grandfather Angelou Rossi and me, Dolly Kyle – 1934

Amid the Great Depression, my Grandfather had a pawn shop and jewelry store. However, business was very slow, so my Grandmother and I would go and stand in line for hours waiting to receive food. And yet, Grandmother was known about the neighborhood as the good woman who fed bums. In fact, someone marked an X on our house to indicate to the homeless that it was a good spot to eat. Grandmother always said, "Soup on the shelf is better than money in the bank." It was the early 30s and it was bad times. The banks closed and you couldn't get your money out to buy any groceries.

One day during these desperate times, my Mother spoke to one of the lady judges at Grandmother's workplace about how she might get enough food for her and me and my grandparents. The judge told my Mother to go on the street and sell herself for food. Now, Italians don't get mad, they get even. So, my Mother got acquainted with the judge's son, who happened to be Jewish. She talked him into getting the keys to the courthouse, where the food was stored. One night my Mother and he took his pick-up truck and got a load of groceries for all of us.

Mother went with this fellow for quite a long time, but they could never marry as he was

Jewish and she Catholic. I remember he had an electrical store with chandeliers and he bought me toys and a little car with pedals so I could go up and down the sidewalk.

Grandmother told me a little of her life. . .how she had dated Grandfather, and they got pregnant with my Mother—Myrtle. But he didn't want to marry her, so he talked his friend Eddie into a union. Grandmother and Eddie married and they had two sons—Melvin and Sonny. Interestingly enough, Grandmother and Eddie remained close friends with Grandfather through the years, right up until the time of Eddie's untimely death in an automobile accident. When my Mother was 12-years-old, her mother and biological father—my Grandmother Edna and Grandfather Angelo— finally were married.

One of my earliest memories of my Grandfather is from when I was about three. He would come home late at night, with Chinese food in tow. As soon as he opened the door, I could smell it. I would stand up in my crib and take in a deep breath. I've always loved Chinese food ever since.

I have wondered over the years of an incident in which I watched my Grandfather sneak in the house and put something in the claw feet of our bathtub; I never knew what he was hiding.

I'm pretty confident much of his business dealings were in the Black Market. In fact, I think he spent a little time in prison at one point or another. I remember we had a big, grand chandelier in our house. It just shimmered. Grandfather reminded us, on numerous occasions, in an urgent sort of way, that if the cops ever came by the house, that we were not to turn on the lights of the chandelier. Turns out, some of the pieces of it were real diamonds!

Around this time I was put in a Catholic childcare center during the day. The nuns were tough. There were white tablecloths on the lunch table. If you spilled milk or anything on the table, you got a whipping. After a couple of whippings, I learned to be careful with my food.

At 6, I was placed in a Catholic school. We wore navy-colored uniforms that consisted of pleated skirts and a white sailor top with a navy-blue tie. They really looked nice. My Grandmother would pin a piece of asphidity to my underwear to keep me from getting any diseases at school. Apparently, asphidity—at least that's what Grandmother called it—was an old-fashioned, home-remedy, preventive medicine. I don't know what all was in the concoction, but it ended up in the form of a dark brown firm piece, with the consistency and look of hardened molasses. Grandmother folded it into a piece of Bull Durham sack and attached the awful thing to me. I guess it smelled so bad that no one came close enough to pass their germs!

Grandmother Edna and me, Dolly Kyle – 1934

We called the incidents my Mother had with her epilepsy, spells, not fits. Dogs had fits. I just remember them happening often, and we all just seemed to get through them calmly. It was just a regular part of our daily lives. Still, she was a beautiful woman. At 20 years old, with a head full of black, curly hair, she came in third in the Miss Sacramento pageant. My Mother was married five times in my first few years of life. Her last marriage was to a man by the name of George Class, whom I always referred to as my stepdad. I also always labeled him as a 12th Street bar professional. I never liked George. In fact, he was an asshole. But, I tolerated him. My Mother was married to him for some 60 years, until his death parted them. When I turned 7, (my Mother was 23) we moved with my stepdad to a ranch in Sacramento County near the town of Sheldon, where George had gotten a job as a butcher. Still, we didn't live there very long.

I remember one day when George lowered me down in a bucket into the well on the ranch to dig out the mud. It was so dark and I was very scared. He pulled up the bucket, emptied it and sent me down again. I did that for about four hours and then he pulled me up and we had some food. That night when I went to bed,

I decided I wanted to go back to my Grandpa and Grandma's house in Sacramento. I packed my doll buggy with five of my dolls and put my clothes in a tin suitcase and down the road I went. I got about a mile and here came my stepdad. He put the buggy in the car and made me walk back dragging the tin suitcase. When I got home, he gave me a spanking, and the next day I was in the well again.

After about a week of doing the mud thing, we got some water through to the house. A few months later, we moved from that place and ended up at a house with a large garage on 47th Avenue in Sacramento, just a few miles from my grandparents. I was so relieved to be back, closer to them.

I was a sickly kid. I contracted diphtheria once and lost all of my hair. George said, "I'm getting a goat for you to milk and for you to drink the milk." My gosh, what a stinking goat. But I did milk her and I did drink the milk. If it was really cold, it didn't taste too bad. After about a year I got stronger, as I couldn't stand to drink the milk any longer!

George and my mother - Myrtle - 1937

Nevada

In 1941, when I was 13, George got a job offer in Hawthorne, Nevada, to help build ammunition bunkers. It paid good money. Still, we lived in a tent, and when the wind blew, our food would get full of sand. It was hard for my body to adjust to the dry climate; I had nose bleeds all the time. So my folks decided we had to leave. Around that same time, George got an offer to run a horse slaughterhouse in Yerington, Nevada, about an hour northwest of Hawthorne—which, obviously, defeated the whole purpose of moving in the first place, to a different climate, for me. I suspect, then, that there was another reason—and likely a not-so-honorable reason on George's part—that he was so willing to pack up and leave Hawthorne so impulsively.

Nevertheless, in Yerington, we had a little house with a wood cook stove, and George's work was only about a block away. Yes, we sure were happy to be moved into that house in the summer, after living in a tent for months. My body eventually acclimated to the desert just fine. My mind and soul made the transition even quicker; I simply love the desert. In fact, when I die, I want my ashes to be spread out in the desert—specifically, the Nevada desert—because that's where my heart has always been—I think mostly because of the many good people. So, yes, put me to rest out there amidst the beautiful, sweet-smelling sagebrush, and with the squirrels. I'm just another desert squirrel.

The man who hired my stepdad for the slaughterhouse job also had five meat shops in Oakland and San Francisco, California. His name was Jim Augustine. He always reminded us that he had a sign in the stores that said, "U.S. Inspected Horse Meat for Sale. No Stamps and Cheap." This was during the War, when we had stamps to pay for gasoline, shoes, meat, tires, sugar and butter. The butter, I remember, was white, like lard, but a little packet of yellow coloring came with it. The slaughterhouse and Mr. Augustine's product were very clean. There was a U.S. Inspector on the floor all the time guaranteeing the meat was choice for human consumption. It was quality, clean meat because the horses were from the wild and just ate good, clean sagebrush or hay. This all made Jim Augustine a rich man.

Mr. Augustine hired a man in Winnemucca, Nevada, named Bill, who was a buyer of chicken horses. They were called chicken horses, because before the War—when horses were being used for human consumption—old, lame horses were butchered and made into feed for chickens only.

Bill would buy the horses from everywhere— Wyoming, Montana, wherever— and ship them to Wabuska, Nevada, just 12 miles from Yerington, where the railroad ran. He'd pay two-cents per pound! The horses came by train in box cars, 25 head to a car. We would unload them and drive them to Yerington.

Yes, I said "we." At 13, I got my first job. I was the only girl out there, and by golly, I held my own. What a job that was! It was hot as the devil! When school was in session, I worked on weekends with one other man, but during the summer, I drove horses every day. I got paid $2.50 for the 12-mile drive. When I asked for a raise to $3, my stepdad said he would just find another man to take my place, so I decided to keep the job for the $2.50, as I had to buy my own school clothes. I continued with Yerington Packers for four years. I just learned as I went— a real example of pure on-the-job training!

Whenever one of the Indian workers didn't make it into work, guess who they called upon to fill-in in the Gut Room, skinning horses? You guessed it! I skinned the horses alright, but I could never shoot one, though. Pigs either. I'd hold them while my stepdad cut them.

I didn't have any problem hunting deer, however. I took my first deer when I was 16, while hunting in Paradise Valley. I just had a little pup tent to camp in, and it was really, really cold. I'd make some hot rocks over the fire and put them in my sleeping bag to warm up my bed. The morning of the day we were going to leave, I tossed the rocks out and just threw my bed roll in the back of the vehicle. When I got home and was unpacking and cleaning up from the trip, I was shaking my bed roll, and out came a rattlesnake! Evidently, he had thought it was really, really cold, too, and was just looking for a place to stay warm. Yikes!

If we only had one box car full of horses, it didn't pay to drive them the 12 miles. Or, if it was winter and the snow made for too hard of a trip, it was faster and cheaper to haul the horses on a truck. So, when I went for my driver's license in Yerington, I got my CDL (Commercial Driver's License) so I could haul horses and cattle. It was 1945, and I was 17-years-old. Back then, it was very unusual for a female—and that young—to obtain a CDL.

One time when I was driving about 80 head, a car came by and the jerk behind the wheel was honking his horn, and it spooked the horses. Five head busted out of the herd. I took off to try and cut them off and get them back in line, but, oh gosh, my horse stepped in a gopher hole and tripped, and I went over his head. He fell on top of me, knocking me out for a bit. When I awoke, he was still on top of me. I reached up and hit him hard on the nose and up he came. I had a hell of a time getting back on him, but finally I did. I lost the five head though, and my stepdad said I had to pay for them, but later on there were horses found at Hooten Wells—Mr. Casey's place south of Silver Springs near the Carson River—a good 10 miles from where I first lost them. Mr. Casey and his grandson, Albert, had corralled the horses, and were holding them for us. (Several years later, my first ex-husband, Tom, married Albert's ex-wife, Amy. Now try and keep that straight, why don't you! It just goes to show, it is a small world.) My stepdad told them if they brought them in, he would pay them so much a head. They were much obliged for that opportunity, and so was I, as that meant no money would be taken out of my hide.

I drove horses in the summer and cleaned the slaughterhouse at nights (for $10 a week), but during the winter I would cook for the guys that worked in the slaughterhouse. I was only 15-years-old when I started cooking for a crew of guys. I cooked on a wood stove, and I told them if any of them complained about my cooking, they'd be cooking themselves. One day when I was just pretty tired of that cooking, I thought I'd give myself a break and play a trick on them—so I poured a bunch of salt into the beans. They all came in to eat , and one of the guys took a big bite of the beans and yelled out, "Gosh damn, Dolly, this is too damn salty!" I really thought I was going to get out of the cooking, but then he added, "Oh yes, this is just the way I like it! I sure do like salt." Guess he put the joke back on me; all the guys and I laughed about it.

We had rodeos in Yerington. Can you guess what event I participated in? I rode the bulls! What a scary thing! But, I was young and dumb, so I did it! At one of the rodeos, Slim Pickens was a participant. He was around 25-years-old and just getting started in the movie business, but to us out in the desert, he was just a young man riding broncs. He saw me riding bulls and asked me to go with him to Hollywood. I was only 17-years-old and my folks said, "No!" But I was glad he had asked.

In the 40s, there was a railroad belonging to the very rich Parr family in the town of Mason, Nevada—population of about 500, if that—just a few miles south of Yerington. The Parrs took a liking to me, and invited me to their home in San Francisco. I rode their train to the City and a chauffeur picked me up in a black limo. At only 16 years old, I felt very strange and out of place. They lived on Lake Street in a three-story brick house. I went up to the door and a butler answered, and a maid took my suitcase and jacket. They instructed me to go up to my room and freshen up. Guess what? They had an elevator to the third floor! My room was deco-rated in a Western theme. Boy, it was beautiful! I took my first shower (we never had showers in any house when I was growing up; I'd always bathed in a bathtub). The shower felt great! I then took the elevator back to the main floor, and stepped off into the dining room. Here was a table that I bet was 40-feet long! My gosh, I didn't know what to think. The lady of the house was at one end, the man at the other, and me in the middle. These were rich folk like I'd never known or seen before. They had a host of black waiters and maids and servants. I sure felt funny—kind of uncomfortable—having anybody wait on me. You know the saying, "I felt like a fish out of water?" Well, I felt like a coyote out of the desert, sitting there at that long, fancy table with two adults at each end of the table, and black people standing all around just waiting to pass me the potatoes or something. . .anything. . .in the middle of a big, cosmopolitan city on the coast.

The maid brought my dinner—whatever it was, it was good. I was disappointed that there were no seconds, but couldn't help but smile to myself at the irony of the situation in light of the life lesson my Grandmother had taught me when I was child. She always said, "Dolly, you only get one pass at this world, so make it a good one, because you can't come back for seconds." I knew I probably should have felt like a princess in that elegant home in San Francisco, but somehow, I did not. The Parrs and I sat and talked after dinner, mostly about the horse business, but I was tired after the long day of traveling, so I excused myself a little early and got back into the elevator to go to my third-floor room. I slept well, as I recall, in a very nice bed, but I imagine all I dreamt of that night were the sweet smell of sagebrush and the desert's night skies illuminated by a dense canopy of bright stars.

First thing next morning was breakfast. I had a glass of milk and a glass of orange juice, one strip of bacon and one egg. Good Grief! They certainly were not hearty-enough eaters for me in the big city. After we were finished eating, my hosts announced that the chauffeur would take me to the Cow Palace. I'd heard of the place from my fellow horsemen at various rodeos who talked about the big rodeos at the Cow Palace. I had the chauffeur drop me off at the corrals, and that's mostly where I hung out. The Cow Palace was a fun place to see, but a few hours later, when the chauffeur picked me up and took me to back to the train to take me home to Yerington, I was happy to go. What an experience for a young girl like me.

When I got home, my pet hog, Pat, was waiting for me at the cattle guard, just down the road from my house. That made me smile, and feel like I was back where I belonged. Funny, some 20 years later, my first daughter accused me of naming her after my hog. I tried to reassure her that really, I hadn't. I actually named her after St. Patricia, the patron saint of Naples.

At 17, I also became engaged to a nice Italian boy, named Joe. He was two years older than me. We got to know each other while I helped milk his family's cows. We also had played in the school band together. Speaking of which, I was never very good at the trumpet. My band teacher, Mr. Martin, called me a "tonguer" because I didn't have enough air. He figured out that I pretended to play most of the time; I just pushed the keys a lot. I used Joe's cows as my excuse. I was always late to school and band class because I milked cows earlier in the morning. I remember I could play one song—"Donkey's Serenade."

I loved Joe's family. I got along just right with them. They were my kind of people, as I was quarter Italian, too—at least! Oh, could Joe's mother cook. Authentic Italian food. . .magnifico! I called Joe's father, Papa. I think everybody did. I remember the quirkiest thing about him. . .no matter the weather or the season, Papa always wore long underwear. I just couldn't figure that out, and was so perplexed by it, because afterall, it got damn hot in the Yerington desert in the summertime. So I asked Papa why he wore long underwear year-round, everyday. He answered matter-of-factly, "What keeps the cold out keeps the heat out too!"

Back to California

After five years in Nevada, it was time to move on to another slaughterhouse in Hayward, California. The one in Yerington was closing; the one we were moving to was beef. I hated to leave Yerington as it was a great little town, but my Grandfather had bought a 15-acre place on Jackson Road in Sacramento for my folks and me.

Joe came to visit me in Sacramento, and things were going along alright, until one time when we met each other for a rodeo in Gault, California. We were having a great time, but at one point in the weekend, he was talking to some gal, and I was visiting a bit with a cowboy I knew who was just a friend. Next thing I know, Joe was taking this gal home. Needless to say, we broke up. Joe and I never had sex—we didn't even think of such things in those days, at that young of an age. I never had a ring from him, either, but I did get one of his big rodeo belt buckles. It was a beauty!

Years later, Joe and I reunited as good, life-long friends. I most recently saw him when he invited me and a girlfriend of mine down to Mexico to his birthday party. Joe is a comfort-able farmer, and he paid for everything for the 60 or so people on the guest list. They had in-vited me to their 60th wedding anniversary cel-ebration over in Yerington, too. It was a beau-tiful party. There were more than 200 people there, and Joe picked up the entire tab. Wow. Anyhow, when we arrived at his 84th (I was 82) birthday party in Mexico, Joe's wife, Bessie, said to me that all the other guests were waiting to see the gal who was first engaged to Joe. When my husband Preston and I were up in Idaho in the 80s and 90s, Joe and Bessie came up to vis-it and brought us some onions and garlic they had grown. Still to this day, every October for my birthday, Joe brings me onions and garlic. Now, that is a great friend, don't you think?

I continued working awhile for the slaughter-house in California, but my horse was replaced with a station wagon. I hauled meat to kennels from Sacramento all the way up to Fair Oaks. Grandfather wanted me to go to a business college in Sacramento, which I did, for a year. Grandfather paid for it all. I remember many of my classmates were veterans.

At 18, I went to work for the Department of Employment, where I took dictation all day long for five different gentlemen. I found myself very restless; I worked there for about a year then decided I wanted to work for the telephone office in Sacramento as an operator. But it wasn't too long after that, that I got antsy there, too, and quit. I went to work at Hale's Department Store on K Street as a biller in the bookkeeping department. There were seven of us billers that put out the statements every month; three of us are still alive! I worked there for three years and loved that job.

In 1949, my Grandfather passed away. It was a very sad day for me. I was 20 years old. Grandfather left me $30,000, which was a lot of money in those days. I put it in the bank. When Grandfather died, I lost my father, as far as I was concerned. I never knew my biological father. I barely regarded George worthy of the title of stepdad. And, yes, I called Joe's father "Papa," but everybody did. But, my Grandfather—he was *my* Papa. I loved him so.

"Papa" Angelou – 1934

My First Husband

Not long after Grandfather passed, some friends of the family were talking to me about some nice ex-marine who was working at the post office in Sacramento. They wanted to set me up with a blind date with him. His name was Tom Jones—not the singer! I said OK, but asked that they please not tell him I had inherited the money. They agreed. Tom and I dated for about six months when he proposed. I was in love, and I accepted. I had just turned 21-years-old. We were married in Virginia City, Nevada, in 1950. We had a great honeymoon; we spent the first night in Reno.

A little more than a year into our marriage, I became pregnant. When I was only six-and-a-half months along, I went into labor. It was a stormy night and Tom was out playing cards with some guys. I called a neighbor lady to come and take me to the hospital.

What a night that was! Nurses packed me in ice to try to stop the bleeding, but it didn't help. November 20, 1951, I gave birth to a 2 lb. 12 oz. baby girl. She was so tiny. They put her into an incubator and the doctor told the nurses not to feed her for 48 hours, but late that night, a nurse—I remember her name was Roberta—did give her some sugar and water through an eyedropper. I could tell from how the doctors responded and the nurses took care of my baby and me that it was a miracle that she was alive.

Tom got to the hospital after the birth. He wasn't particularly concerned with the fact that he wasn't with me until then. He said something like, "Well, my mother did it," implying that it was no big deal that I gave birth alone. I snapped back, "Well, that was your mother. Not me!" But, we were one in our deep worry about our daughter. Not hopeful of our little girl surviving, we had a priest administer her last rites. We named her Patti Ann. My tiny baby girl lost weight quickly, going down to a pound-and-a-half. I prayed so hard for her, and kept praying. I went home a week after, but Patti Ann stayed in the hospital; she had to be five pounds before we could take her home. Finally, three months later, the day came when we could take her home. My dear Grandmother was there to help me and Tom. We stayed up night and day, struggling to feed her just an ounce of milk. Oh boy, what a job that was. We kept her on a pillow because if you handled her little body too much, it would get sore. The doctors never had any idea as to why I had her so early. I've often wondered if I went into premature labor because of the work I was doing. We were building onto our house at that time, and maybe my work on the concrete overdid it—I don't know.

About four more months down the road, Patti Ann contracted pneumonia and we had to take her back to the hospital. I went to the Catholic church and prayed and prayed. Incidentally, shortly after Patti was born, Tom and I were inspired to renew our vows in the Catholic church. We got "re-married" in the chapel right across the street from the hospital where Patti Ann had been born, and was now admitted again. While I was praying, Tom came in and told me she was going to be just fine. So, prayers do work.

The bill for her birth alone at Mercy Hospital was $2,000. My husband was working as a hod (brick mud) carrier making $15 a day. We were in debt. One day I was washing the cloth diapers on a washboard. Tom looked over at me and said that if I got pregnant again, he would buy me a wringer washing machine. Not long after, in 1953, I was pregnant. I delivered at seven months this time. It was a boy. Tommy, Jr. weighed only 3 lbs. 4 oz. He was also put into an incubator. He was very strong though and got to five pounds in what seemed like no time, and we brought him home. I remember that his bill was the same as Patti's—$2,000.

When the kids were still tykes, we sold our place and moved to Franklin, Massachusetts, to live with Tom's mother, who was a widow. There was one point pretty early on during the drive out there that the kids got a little rambunctious. I yelled back at them, "If you kids don't quiet down, I'm gonna get a bear to get you!" In Yellowstone, we actually saw a bear. The kids were pretty quiet the rest of the trip!

What a wonderful lady Tom's mother was. Her house was lovely. It was so different from the West, but we really enjoyed living there. It was particularly beautiful in the Fall. I liked that season best out there; the Fall colors were so breathtaking, so beautiful. Near the end of our short stint of three years living back East, my Grandmother came out to visit, and stayed about two months. We all loved having her there. *She* was my Mama. Grandmother passed away shortly after she returned to Sacramento. I am so grateful for that special time we had together in Massachusetts.

My mother Myrtle, "Mama" Edna holding my daughter Patti and me - 1953

Nevada Again

When Grandmother passed in 1956, we flew back to California to help settle her affairs. While we were there, Tom announced that he wanted to go to Fallon, Nevada, and find a place to buy—a ranch, to be more precise. My folks had moved there and lived on a 12-acre ranch on Pasture Road. You ought to have seen the mess he got us into!

While we were driving to Fallon, I kept asking him what kind of house was on the land he had found and purchased on his own. All he would say about it was: "Not bad." Oh, boy! It was a shack! About seven miles out of town, on what came to be known as Solias Road, the place was a mess. A Greek man and his wife had lived there for awhile, and the yard was full of deer horns and hides. The house had four rooms. A path led from there to the outhouse. Honest to God, it was awful. Wouldn't you know—nowadays, some 50 years later—there is a great, big, beautiful house out there.

Forty acres, some corrals and a couple of run-down sheds full of junk and Tom had dumped all our money into this place, so we didn't have much choice but to start cleaning it up. I went into the house and scrubbed it clean with Clorox, and then I wall-papered the supposed walls, and scoured the kitchen. The floors were all wavy. I knew I was lucky to have water in the house, even though it was an old-fashioned hand pump. We had to buy a propane refrigerator, but we already had a wood-and-propane stove from my Grandmother's belongings, so that was a blessing.

We had a light plant with a gasoline engine that had to be primed to get working so we could have light, so we also had a kerosene lamp on hand. The light plant was about 20 feet from this so-called house, in a root cellar full of spiders. And of course, we had an outside toilet—that was fun. Not!

Five months had passed and it was necessary for Tom to find a job as we had just about depleted our savings. But first, Tom said, the tractor had broken down and he needed to go to Reno, about an hour west of Fallon, to find a part for it. I told him to take only $100 and, please Tom, I said, "Don't gamble." So off he went. He didn't come home for three days. I knew right away he had lost what we had. He blew the $100 and three hundred more. It was all we had. I was really pissed at him.

I didn't want to do anything yet, as far as asking my folks for help. So, we went along for a little while longer, somehow, but Tom couldn't find a job, and we were hungry. A couple down the road from us was having a hard time too, so the man and Tom got together and decided to kill a cow out in the desert. It belonged to someone else, but we were hungry. They cleaned it and hung it over at the man's house. We were scared to death that someone was going to see it and we'd all be in jail.

More time went by, and still, no job. My folks loaned me money for food, so Tom decided to take the money and go to town to look for a job. And he got one, as a bartender, at the Keystone Club on Maine Street. I was so relieved and I finally started to relax and be happy living in that shack, taking care of the kids. Tom was making decent money. But about a month later, he came home drunk. I was so damned upset, I told him to go to hell, and I took the kids and went to stay at my folks' place. Our divorce was final in 1956.

Immediately I went out and found myself a job at Kent's Butcher Shop on Maine Street. I worked a few days a week in the office of Kent's Grocery Store, too. I worked my butt off, as it was important to me to pay my mom to take care of my children. I didn't have a car to get back and forth to work. I found a piece of junk that had no door on the driver's side for eighty bucks. I asked my parents to borrow $80, but they said they didn't have it. I was telling a girl-friend how I needed a car, and about the ol' clunker I had found. My friend—her name was Pepper—said, "I have $80 in the bank you can have, Dolly." I told her I would pay her back in two weeks. I was working seven days a week, so I was able to pay her back just when I said I would. I worked in that damned cold butcher shop all winter long. My door-less car wasn't any warmer, but it ran fine.

Husband Number Two

In 1959, I was working at the Bank Club, and that is where and when I met my second husband, Zigmont Magiera. And like my first husband, Zig was a military man, too. He was stationed at the naval base in Fallon when we met. (Incidentally, out of my six husbands, four were military men: Tom was a Marine, Zig was Air Force, Wayne was Navy, and Preston was Air Force. I guess I've always been a pretty patriotic gal, eh?) Zig, originally from Massachusetts, was about 40-years-old, and I was near 30. I told him I had two children, but he said he didn't mind that, and he kept coming in to see me.

One Sunday morning Zig came by to pick me and my kids up to take us for a long drive. Zig and I went together for about six months when he proposed to me. I was ready, so we married in 1959, and the kids and I moved in with him into a nice, little house on the naval base. Patti was about 8 years old and Tommy was 6.

It was good to be married to a nice man. Zig only drank a little, but certainly was no drunk. We had a good life. I soon got pregnant with my third and last child. A baby girl—Andrea— joined our family in late 1960. She was born at Churchill County Hospital in Fallon and weighed a whopping (comparatively-speaking!) 7 lb. 4 oz.—the biggest baby I had. I was so big when I was pregnant. One time when I was about seven months along, I fell into the deep freeze out in the shed. Thank goodness it was full, as I had a hell of a time anyhow getting up out of there with my big belly. The doctors said I wasn't built to have such a large baby, so they took her two weeks early by Caesarean section. The births of my first two kids each cost $2,000. This one was $25. Thank God for the United States Air Force.

We lived in Fallon for about six more months and then Zig received orders to a strategic air command (SAC) base in Marysville, California. We lived in a really nice duplex on base. I remember bathing Andrea in the kitchen sink there—it was just easier and more comfortable for the both of us. I also remember making lots of friends there even though I was told by some higher-ups that I shouldn't associate with non-commissioned families. I didn't listen very well, and just responded with something like, "I'm not in the service, my husband is." We liked living there a lot—Patti and Tommy were doing well in school—but we ended up not being there very long—only about six months—before Zig was transferred back to Fallon. Not long after that, he retired from the Air Force, and we made a plan to settle in Fallon. Zig didn't go back to work for quite a while, but eventually he had to. He picked up odd jobs around Fallon, but it ended up that that just wasn't fulfilling enough for Zig, and he started drinking more, and then, much out of character for him, he started drinking too much. He became unreasonably strict with Patti and Tommy—like, for instance, he would not allow them to have ketchup on their hamburgers. I don't know what that was all about, but needless to say, he and I grew apart. It wasn't too long after we moved back to Fallon, that we separated. I took the three kids and rented a three-bedroom, one-bath house with my girlfriend, Nadine, on Virginia Street. She had two little boys of her own. It was early 1962.

I worked for a time at Eddie's Barbecue, a joint on Maine Street. Eddie had 10-cent beer, wine and whiskey, and 10-cent craps. I tended bar and cooked hamburgers and hotdogs. Eddie was one tough asshole to work for. He told me how much fries to use—just a small handful. I did what he asked, making $1 an hour.

One day a customer came in with his two sons, and I served them. He was talking to me about Leno's Dinner House in town. It set on the middle of Williams Avenue, about where Taco Bell is today. He said a woman, by the name of Jane, ran the restaurant and she needed a waitress. Another day, not long after this customer's visit, a man came in and ordered a hamburger and fries. I went right to preparing his order. I grabbed a big handful of fries. Eddie came over and chewed me out about the amount of fries again, and called me a choice name. I turned around and said to him, "You can take these fries and shove them up your ass. I quit!" I went straight over to Leno's and talked to that gal Jane. She hired me on the spot.

Leno's was a great place to work, and Jane was a fine woman to work for. She looked just like Olive Oyl (remember Popeye's girlfriend, Olive Oyl?), and she knew it; she showed off her long legs. I made $2 an hour, plus tips—good tips. I was so happy. I worked six nights as a waitress, and then on Monday nights, I filled in for the cook so she could have a day off. Looking back, I really appreciated working for a woman, especially one as sharp and sensible as Jane. She was innovative. She came up with the technique of serving salads off of a Lazy Susan. It went off real well. Unfortunately, too soon after I started working for her, Jane got sick and couldn't work anymore.

Jane ordered supplies from a local, small grocery store run by a guy named Larry. I got acquainted with Larry over time, when he made deliveries, about three times a week. One time, he brought me a bottle of champagne. "Wow," I said, "I've never drunk that before." But, sometime later, on a Monday night after Jane had left, I got into the champagne. I had just finished cutting the fat off of a top sirloin and put it into a pan and into the oven. I kept on drinking the champagne and forgot the fat in the oven. All of a sudden, the pan caught on fire! I told Millie, the waitress, to go to over to the gas station next door and get a fire extinguisher. She didn't find one, and even though I had managed to get the oven turned off, smoke still began to billow into the dining room full of people. I told Millie if they complained to tell them I burnt a steak, which she did. Leno was tending bar, but somehow never seemed to know what had had happened. I was glad when that shift was over!

One night after I got off shift, I decided to go down to Stockman's to see my gal friend, Alice Warner, who was a dealer there, and to have myself a relaxing drink. Soon after I sat down, John, the bartender, came over to me and said the gentleman at the end of the bar wanted to buy me a drink. I said, "OK," and when I got my drink, I raised my glass to the man as a gesture of thanks. Pretty soon, the man came down and sat next to me. It was Larry, the delivery guy, from Leno's. We spent awhile talking and laughing, when all of a sudden the front door opened and in came a big woman. She walked right up to Larry and me, got between us, and hit him across his face so hard, it knocked his glasses off of his head! Then she caught me on the up-swing! She turned around and walked out. I yelled at Larry, "Who was that?" He answered, "That is my wife." I yelled again, "Oh my god! You didn't say you were married!" I noticed Larry didn't seem too surprised or too bothered by the curious turn of events. But, I kind of liked him. So, I decided, being the Italian I am, that I wouldn't get mad, I'd just get even. . .I reeled him in, and went with him for the next three years!

A Love Affair

Larry and I were into our affair about a year when he bought me a two-karat diamond ring. It was beautiful. One day, though, when I was visiting a girlfriend at her house, Larry came over and demanded the ring back, as he was mad at me for talking to another male sales-man who had come in at Leno's. He chased me around that house, trying to get the ring. My girlfriend had some plants setting all around her house. At one point, I ran ahead of Larry and stuck the ring in one of those plants. When he finally caught me—no ring! He asked me what happened to it and I said it must have fallen off my finger. He didn't seem like he believed me, but still, he left the house.

I went back and found the ring and put it right back on my finger. Larry never said another word about it, and we kept on seeing each other for another couple of years. (Some years later, after we broke up, I sold that ring and bought myself a pick-up truck!)

One time Larry was going over to Winnemucca to a golf tournament, and he wanted me to join him for the weekend. I spent the majority of the time in our hotel room, calling room service plenty, because most of the guys Larry was golfing with were from Fallon, and all I needed was for them to see me anywhere around Larry. On the last night of the tournament though, the guys took off for Fallon, so Larry and I went to a nice restaurant and had a great dinner with champagne, then headed home to Fallon ourselves. It was a beautiful moonlit night. Larry decided we should stop and talk awhile. Talk?—Yeah, right! He pulled out into the desert by some railroad track. I said to him, "I don't feel right, Larry. I don't think we should be here in the moonlight. You can see the truck from the highway." I was uneasy, so we left. Just before we got into town, we saw his wife. I told him to drop me off and that I'd get a cab home. My suitcase was in the backseat of his pickup, so I reminded him to lock the back door on the truck so no one could get into it—namely, his wife. When I got back to my folks' place, I asked my stepdad to go down to Larry's store—an old Farmer's Market that used to be way out on Reno Highway, across from where WalMart now stands—to get my suitcase. Wow, that was one close call! Still, I've always said, "Married men are safer, because you don't have to do their laundry!"

Larry frequently took me to the better places out of town. One time we took my two friends with us and went to a place between Reno and Carson City called The Lancers. It was a beautiful restaurant up on a hill. It was snowing. We had steak and champagne, and we all had a great time. Larry and I had a ball dancing.

Another time Larry said he and a bunch of his buddies were driving to my ol' stompin' grounds of Sacramento to play golf. He bought me a ticket to fly down there and also gave me some spending money. He had reservations at a big, fancy hotel—the Senator Hotel. I took a taxi there from the airport, got into our room and showered. Larry called me to say we would be having dinner at the hotel when he got back from playing golf. It was a beautiful dining room. It made me reminiscent of the Parr Family's big dining room that I sat at as a young girl only 15 years or so before. My, how life changes.

While Larry and I were having dinner, we

heard some music, and asked the waiter what was going on. He said it was a private party. When we finished our dinner, Larry declared, "We are going in there." We not only crashed that party, but Larry also paid the band $50 to play our song, "Fascination." We started dancing and the people in there stood back and watched us. We danced really well together. After the music stopped, they applauded. I felt strange because we weren't even invited guests, but it was a lot of fun. The next day I hopped on a plane and flew back to Reno.

Christmas 1963, Larry bought me a new car— a steel-gray Bonneville. I had never had a new car before. I didn't know until years later that Larry had also bought his wife a new car at the same time. I thought that was great! Larry was so good to me and I loved him, but we drifted apart after awhile. He and his wife leased the golf course in Fallon and gradually he didn't have time for me.

A Movie-Star Sighting

About this time, I went to work at the Palace Club as a change girl and also did some bartending and cashiering as well. One night a tall man came into the Palace Club—a movie star named Joel McCrea. He and another man sat down at the counter to have a sandwich. Mr. McCrea came up to pay his bill. As he was walking out, I was paying attention to him (he was so good looking!) and I caught my middle finger in the cash register drawer. I didn't yelp out in pain like I wanted to, so McCrea was none the wiser, (thank goodness!), that I practically lost a finger over him! Boy, did that hurt! I reported it to the cook, and since my finger was already swelling up, he told me to go to the doctor, who diagnosed that he would have to take the top of my finger off. . .without anesthesia. I said, "No Way!" Dr. Shambeau was known to have no mercy for no body! When I balked, he said, like only a man would, "Well, you had a couple of kids, didn't you?" Instead, I went over to the Sagebrush Club and downed a fifth of brandy, and then I asked Forrie, the bartender, for an extra shot. He asked, "Why do you need that?" I held up my bulging finger (it was my middle finger, conveniently-so, I thought) and said, "This is why!" I went back and had my finger cut, drained and bandaged. I was in the hospital for a day, then I was right back to work. Boy, did all that ever hurt, but it was worth it, I thought, just to get a chance to see Joel McCrea up close.

A Lot of Pancakes

Not too long after my movie-star-sighting-slashed-finger incident, I started working at the Bank Club in Fallon, a small restaurant that had a bar, slots and Keno. I was the chief cook and bottlewasher and waitress. Every morning, a cop by the name of Don would come in for his "free coffee." After about a month, the cop says to me, "You know Dolly, sometimes we have a bunch of seasonal Mexican workers come in here to have breakfast." I said I thought that would be OK, afterall, that is why I was there as a cook. I didn't know it at the time, but Don was setting me up.

So, one morning around 3 a.m., the bar phone rang at the Bank Club, and Tex the bartender yelled out, "It's for you, Dolly! Bring your pad and pencil." Turns out, Tex was in on the whole caper, too. I took the order over the phone; the person on the other end talked with a Mexican accent. He said he was bringing in a bunch of Mexicans for breakfast in a few hours. He wanted to order ahead of time. I said OK, and he proceeded to order 30 stacks of pancakes! About this time, I was getting nervous. That was 90 damn pancakes! Plus scrambled eggs, coffee, and bacon or ham. He said they would all be in around 5 a.m. That was less than two hours away! My god, I was nervous! I hung up the phone and Tex said, "Dolly, I'll help you." I shot back, "I hope so."

I went back into the kitchen and found a 25-lb. bag of pancake mix. We had a big mixer—thank goodness for that!—and I dumped the whole damn bag in the mixer—poured in water and salad oil and started mixing. I worked furiously. I was walking on pins and needles, and I thought Tex was probably walking on eggshells. Five o'clock came round, and there was no sign of anybody. I said to Tex, "Where in the hell are those Mexicans?" Unbeknownst to me, Tex strained to keep a straight face as he reassured me, "They will be here." More time passed, and I anxiously exclaimed to Tex that I was going to get fired for mixing up all that pancake flour.

About that time, here walks in that damned cop, Don. And he just started laughing, and so did Tex. I didn't think it was so damn funny. I called them both a son of a bitch! But still, I was so worried that I was going to get fired. At 6 a.m., the boss arrived. I wasted no time telling him what happened. He said, "That's OK, Dolly, we will use up the pancake mix. I am not going to fire you." I was happy and relieved, but at that point, I was exhausted and numb, too, from all the work and worrying I'd been doing. But that was OK, because, remember: I knew, Italians don't get mad, they get even. . . Indeed! I just didn't know it would be a red-and-silver blouse and a wetsuit that would help me with my plan of revenge.

There was a short period of time when a young man by the name of Rob kept coming in and talking to me while I was working. He was nice, and one night, right around the same time Don and Tex had had their fun with me, Rob said to me, "How would you like to go with me to Lake Tahoe to go scuba diving?" I didn't know what he meant, but I was game to try. He told me where he lived and to be at his house at 9 a.m. the next day.

It was Sunday, my day off. When I got to his house, Rob gave me a present. It was a beautiful red blouse with silver in it. I couldn't believe it.

I asked him what it was for, exactly; he just told me to go into the bedroom and put it on. Turned out, he had the same shirt on, so we looked like twins.

We got into his beautiful Cadillac and headed for Tahoe. We stopped at a few places along the way. We had lunch and a few drinks; I was feeling no pain. I still didn't know about this scuba diving thing, but as I said, I was game. We got to Tahoe and he drove down to a spot, lakeside. He handed me a wetsuit and instructed me to go into the bushes and put it on. My gosh! It was like putting on a damn tight girdle. Next, Rob came up and told me to get down on my knees. He put a tank on my back and some other scuba stuff like a lead weight belt, the mouthpiece for air, a round glass mask, and fins on my feet. There I was—looking just like that guy from Sea Hunt!

It was only then that I made mention of the minor detail that I didn't know how to swim! Rob said, "That's OK, the tank will hold you up and the fins will help." I was scared of deep water, but I tried following him into the lake. With all the stuff I had on, plus the heavy tank, I couldn't move! So I got down on all fours and crawled to the water. I must have looked very funny.

Rob was a little ways ahead of me, and he kept waving for me to follow him. It was definitely beautiful there; the water, crystal clear. I went out far enough to go under but something inside told me that was as far as I wanted to go. Rob kept waving at me to follow him out further and deeper. I thought to myself, "I'm high-tailing it back to dry ground," which I did. I doggie-paddled my way back to shore. On the way back though, I saw a crawdad on the lake bottom. I pulled out a knife that was in the weight belt and stabbed the creature and took it along home with me. I was very happy to get my sea legs back on dry land. I took off the gear in the bushes, put my red-and-silver blouse back on, and waited peacefully for Rob to come back in.

On the way home, we stopped and had a great dinner with wine. Rob never made any advances toward me, for which I was grateful. We had a really nice time that day, I thought. That evening, he dropped me off at Frankie's Club on the north end of Maine Street, and I never saw him again. Sometime later, after that day, I found out Rob was gay.

Now, about that crawdad. . .

You see, Don the cop—you know, my little practical-joker friend—used to go fishing with Willie Capucci. Everybody knew Willie. He is the guy who owned the house that used to have all the ducks in the pond in front, on South Taylor across from the bowling alley. Willie did a lot for the town, like he always provided the loudspeaker system for parades. He was always doing something for someone, even strangers. Unfortunately, his generosity was the death of him. Some young man he had helped out, turned on Willie. The hoodlum went back to Willie's house and murdered him over borrowed money. What a tragedy. Anyhow, every time Don and Willie went fishing, apparently, Don would inevitably hook a crawdad on his line. He'd have Willie take the critter off, as he was scared of crawdads. (I know! This is a cop we are talking about!)

So, a few days after I got back from Tahoe, I still had that crawdad in my bag. And I knew what time Don made his rounds. In he came to Frankie's, about 4 a.m. I made sure to make a show of fiddling with something in my bag. Don asked me what I had in the bag. I answered innocently, "Do you really want to see this, Don?" He said assuredly, "Yes!" This was the time for the Italian to get even. He came up close to look in the bag and I reached in and got hold of the crawdad and pushed it into Don's face. He screamed and ran out of the bar! I was right behind him with the crawdad in my hand, running down Maine Street, chasing a cop. He finally out-ran me, but I was quite happy and satisfied that I had gotten him back.

Deputy for a Day

That wasn't the first time in my life that I, shall we say, "served and assisted" law enforcement. It was back in 1958 when I was Deputy for a Day!

I was living with my folks on Soda Lake Road, when one day the Indian sheriff came to the ranch and asked if I had a gun. I answered, of course, yes. He wanted me to ride out with him to gather up some kids who had broken out of a juvenile work camp out in the desert around Schurz. (Schurz is the little village—a Paiute Indian Reservation, in fact—30 minutes south of Fallon.) He stated, "Well, I know you can ride." I went out and got my horse saddled and hopped up on it. The sheriff instructed me to put my left hand on the Bible he had, and to raise my right. He was ready to deputize me. I thought to myself, "Wow, this is serious." The delinquents we were after had broken into a ranch on Cox Road, stole the owner's guns and ammunition, and then just started shooting the place up. When we got to the house, the owner was lying on the floor.

The Sheriff and I headed down Cox Road in search of those rogue kids. There were some big tamarack bushes across the road from the shot-up house. The sheriff told me to go rustle around those big bushes to see if the kids would flush out. He said he was going to head out onto the desert to see if anything was going on.

I rode around the bushes, gun in my hand, yelling, "Come out with your hands up!" Nothing happened. Whew, I was happy about that! So, I rode out in the desert to see if I could meet up with the sheriff, but he was nowhere to be found.

I saw some dust in a gully and although scared, rode slowly up to it. I found a guy on a motorcycle. I told him to leave because there were some mean kids out there somewhere carrying guns. So he took off.

I rode around for about 30 minutes more and then headed back home to the ranch. I was home for about an hour when the sheriff came back to report that the kids were apprehended way out on the Lovelock Highway. I was glad. That ended my day as a deputy.

For years there has been a big rodeo in Fallon called the All-Indian Stampede. During this weekend, Frankie's was always jumpin'! I was working this one night with my friend Claudia when I spotted a bunch of beer cans on the table by the wall. As I grabbed a bar towel, I told Claudia over my shoulder that I was going over to clean up those cans. On my way over, I came across a very large male Indian passed out on the floor. I just stepped over him and started picking up the cans and wiping up the stinking beer that had spilled out of them. My bar towel was soaked heavy with beer, and I said to myself, "Hmm, what an opportunity this is!" I wrung that bar towel right out into the mouth of that passed-out Indian. He came right up, and looked about 6' 5" inches tall. He glared down at me and my 5' 5" frame. Out the back door I ran! I ran past the police station, around on Williams Avenue, around the gas station on the corner and then back to the bar. I lost him, thank goodness. I walked slowly into the bar and Claudia said, "My god, Dolly, I thought he caught you." What a run that was!

Clowning Around, Some Drama, and Santa

"Dolly the Clown"
Painting by my dear friend,
the late Merry Jo Converston

When I wasn't clowning around, as usual, I was clowning around, seriously, if that's possible. I played a clown for years in Fallon at various children's parties, at golf course events, and in plenty of parades. I was a rodeo clown, too. One year, when the rodeo was at the Fallon fairgrounds, I, of course, had had a few drinks. My daughter and three of her girlfriends were walking in front of the Dry Gulch Bar and one of the gals said as they passed, "Look there is a clown swinging from the rafters." My daughter said, "Oh my god, it's my mother." She was not happy with me.

My third husband, Wayne, found the predicaments I got myself into, mixing clowning and drinking, pretty humorous. We'd only been married three days when I served as clown for a parade in town. After the parade, two of my friends—Edie and Dorothy—took me to Stockman's. I remained in my clown costume, and good gosh was it ever hot. I had a few drinks— OK, I was pretty much plastered—and got so unbearably hot, I could hardly stand it. So I told the girls I had to get home and get out of that damn suit and get my makeup off because it had begun to itch like crazy. The girls took me home. I went straight to the kitchen table and passed out, but not before I ripped off the clown suit. That is as far as I got. So, there I was, just lying there in nothing but my panties. . .and, oh yes, my clown face makeup. That must've been quite a sight; a nudist clown! At some point, Wayne apparently came in, took one look at me and laughed his head off, and then just left me there. He told me about it later. Maybe an hour later, I eventually came to, and felt sick, sick, sick. Still, I headed for the shower, and got ready for work. I was one sick cookie, but still I had to pour drinks all night. Needless to say, I was not a happy camper. . .or maybe it'd be more accurate to say I was not a happy clown! I did wash off my makeup in the shower, by the way!

My schedule at Frankie's got to where I was mostly tending bar on the dayshift, so it was usually pretty quiet for me. Until the day Hell's Angels rolled in. Before they arrived, I had two male customers sitting at the end of the bar. About 10 a.m. the doors flew open and here come a band of Hell's Angels, more than a dozen of them. Their bikes filled the street out front. Oh my, was I ever nervous. I asked the two guys who had been there, to stay. I even offered to buy their beer. But they gave me an emphatic "No Way!" and out the door they went. The Hell's Angels ordered drinks. I was down at the end of the bar, working on filling the orders, when one of those hellions reached over and jerked me by my blouse right up over and onto the bar, yelling, "I'm going to get you, lady!" I was able to reach behind the bar right to where I knew the ice pick lay. I got hold of it and came around and stabbed it right into his hand. He screamed out in pain and let loose of me. I told him to peacefully go into the men's room and wash off his hand and then I'd pour some whiskey over it. He did as I said. I had no more problems with any one of them from that group for the rest of the day. They stayed until about three that afternoon.

I had worked at Frankie's for some time, the second-time around, when one night, in came my ol' lover, Larry. . .with his wife, Nellie. She was revved up and in quite a mood. Obviously, she had somehow learned about my and Larry's past. I had seen her once before, when Larry and I first met, when she walloped us both, but I did not remember her being such a large, husky woman. Good gosh, she was big enough to eat hay with a pitchfork! I was just waiting for her to come around behind the bar and hit me again. I held a bottle of liquor in my hand, just in case, but Larry got up and talked her into going outside. I was so relieved.

I actually did see Nellie again, on much better terms, some 10 or more years later, after Larry had passed. I had played Santa during Christmas time for years, and one year, for some reason, I decided to go by and visit Nellie in my Santa costume. She knew who I was; I was surprised she let me in. We sat and drank some wine together and talked about Larry. He had passed away in 1978. She asked me, "Did Larry ever buy you a mink coat?" I said no, and I didn't make any mention of the car or the diamond. Ironically, Nellie and I became friends. She even kept in touch with me years later, when I lived in Palm Springs. She'd call me, religiously, once a week.

Yes, for years, I played Santa Claus every Christmas throughout the community. One year, Santa made the rounds, via taxicab, to the rest homes in Fallon. Oh, what a place to go. It was very sad for me to see people in those homes that I had known for years; one friend of mine ended up being in for 18 years. It just broke my heart. I'd come out of each home, just a bawling. The cab driver would say to me, "I've never seen Santa cry." I sobbed, "You just go in there for awhile. You'll come out crying too."

The last time I was Santa, I arrived by helicopter. The pilot—named Chris Palludan—was Santa's helper, The Elf. (Chris was actually the person who hired me to play Santa.) We landed in the parking lot of Kent's Grocery. That part was a little scary for both Santa and The Elf, but overall, we had so much fun. We really enjoyed the kids.

Husband Number Three

In 1963 I met a handsome man named Wayne Workman. He was a bartender and a barber. We had been seeing each other for about six months when he wanted to get married. I was game. Even though we were ancient history, Larry was upset with me and asked if I was going to marry "that man." I said yes, I most certainly was.

Wayne and I got married at some friends' house in Fallon, and went to Coeur d'Alene, Idaho, for our honeymoon, where I met his sister and brother. We stayed there for about two weeks, then headed home to Fallon. The five of us—Wayne, me and the kids—lived in a small apartment by Oats Park. Wayne opened a barber shop in Fernley, a little town just a half-hour to the east, between Fallon and Reno. We had that shop for about a year. On Sundays and Mondays, Wayne tended bar to make extra money at the Wagon Wheel, way out on the south side of Reno Highway, almost to the junction where it turns off to Lahontan Reservoir. That old building is still standing.

Idaho

In the early 60s, we decided to move to Coeur d'Alene, Idaho. What a beautiful

place. We rented a two story house from Wayne's sister. It was very nice; the kids had the whole upstairs and lots of room. We were happy there.

Both of us had to find jobs. And we both did, at the same place—a country club at Hayden Lake. My sister-in-law babysat the kids while I worked as a waitress for $1 an hour, and Wayne bartended. It was a beautiful place to work. We were doing quite well and were quite content, which makes me think, and chuckle, about how people always insinuated I was wild in regards to why I married so many times. I'd answer back without hesitation, "Two paychecks are better than one!" Hell, I had three kids to support. I was making $1/hour for a long time before I was bumped up to just $2. It was tough. That's why I got married so many times. And, I loved all of my husbands, but I was in love with only one of them.

My first day on the job started at about 5 p.m. I immediately got a table with a party of four. These guests were regulars, and the other waitresses were familiar with their demeanor, and thought they would be a good group for me to start out with.

This restaurant served its baked potatoes in foil, but none of the other waitresses remembered to tell me that one of the guests in my party did not like his baked potato served that way, and that I should take the foil off his potato before bringing it to the table. As I walked away from the table, this asshole threw that potato at me and hit me in the middle of my back. They were the only people in the restaurant at the time. I didn't miss a step; I picked up that potato and threw it back at him and it hit him in the head and fell to pieces. As I lobbed the potato, I said to myself, "Oh boy, I'm going to be fired before I even get started." But when I went to take them their check, the customer said to me, "Girl, you are the first one who has ever stood up to me. Here is your tip." Guess what? He gave me a twenty dollar bill. I almost fainted. That size of a tip was unheard of in those days. What's more, most rich people are lousy tippers. I came to understand that none of the other waitresses had ever received that kind of tip from him.

One Saturday night, we held a luau at work. Each of us servers was given these gorgeous leis of orchids to wear. Wow! I just loved mine. The chef had arranged for an octopus for an elaborate centerpiece. I'll tell you, I'd never seen anything like that! He covered the tentacles with mashed potatoes and parsley, and put a crown of some sort on its head. It was really different. The chef also ordered several ice sculptures. The whole spread was pretty fancy.

Our boss told us we could dance with the members, i.e. the older men. But no drinking by employees was allowed. Each man I danced with asked if he could buy me a drink and I said, "We can't drink, but why don't you buy me that drink and put it in the men's card room." By the time I was finished dancing that night, there must have been 30 drinks waiting for me in the card room. I discreetly spread the word to a few of my fellow waitresses, and we all went to the card room. A couple of busboys joined us, too. They were only 18. We sat and drank all those pineapple rum drinks with the little umbrellas in them. I guess we were in there for at least two hours, then the other waitresses went home. But, I stayed. . .for I, of course, had a plan.

I talked one of the busboys into staying and helping me. I told the kid, "Let's get that octopus." What can I say?—You do strange things when you are drunk. The kid said back to me, "What for?" I told him I just wanted it. So we hauled it out and put it into the trunk of my car. We headed for Lake Coeur d'Alene. We washed the potatoes off and then laid it on the shore. I took the busboy home, and then I went home. The next day's headlines in the Coeur d'Alene paper? "Octopus Washes Up On Shore." Of course, everyone knew it was a joke because it was a fresh water lake, but neither I nor the busboy ever said a word. Of course I had threatened him not to. I know. Crazy. But it was pretty damned funny too.

I did questionably "brave" things when I was drunk. One time, some years after the Octopus incident, my gal friend, Rowena and I closed up a bar in Fallon at two in the morning, and starting walking home in the snow. The cold flakes were coming down like the devil. The streets were empty except for a lone semi I saw coming down the main street. I dared Rowena to stop the truck, climb up into the cab and kiss that trucker. She declared that she was not going to do any such thing, but then turned around and dared me to do it. Well, you know me and dares, or anything that resembles one! So, I got out into the street and waved my hands. The truck stopped and I climbed up into the cab—oh! It was so warm in there!— and I kissed that handsome trucker. I told him it was a dare. He didn't care what the reason was and suggested we get in the back sleeper. I said No, and climbed back down out of the cab. The trucker drove on, and Rowena and I—despite my dangerous, little game—went home safely to sleep in our own warm beds.

I kept working at the country club, for a year, in fact, but it wasn't too long that Wayne got tired of tending bar, so he went back to cutting hair. One day I went to work and my boss said she had a catering job for me and a bartender at a home on the golf course. The customer was hosting a barbecue for about 40 guests. We had to haul some dishes and liquor over to the home.

Well, the party barely got started when it became obvious that the host was toasted and incapable of barbecuing the chicken. So, guess who had to do it? I cooked and served all of the guests. What a job that was. The bartender was serving drinks and I saw the host give him a $20 bill. I was thinking I was going to get more than that because of all that I had done. Well, we got everything cleaned up and put away and as I was leaving, the host gave me a measly $5 bill. I was pissed. I told the guy to keep his damn five dollar bill, as he needed it more than I did. When we got back to the club, I told my boss not to ever send me on another catering job. It wasn't long after that, though, that I quit.

I got another job, but it was 25 miles from Coeur d'Alene. It was at a floating dinner house called the Golden Hind—a beautiful place right on Lake Pend Oreille by Ponderay, Idaho. My first night, the place was full. I had a party of six who wanted drinks before dinner. They were all decked out in tuxedoes and evening gowns. I was carrying their drinks to the table and all of a sudden a damn speedboat went by and rocked the dinner house. We already know that I don't have sea legs; I lost my tray of drinks all over those people. Oh my! I felt so bad, and I apologized over and over to them. "Here I go again," I thought. "Getting fired before I even begin!" I told them that if I made any tips that night,

I would pay for their dry-cleaning. They were so understanding. They told me it was OK—it wasn't my fault. The rest of the night went pretty well; I made good tips, and I didn't have to pay for the dry-cleaning afterall.

The second night I had a table of six for dinner. I served them their dinner and all went well with that. But then came the dessert. The ice cream was out back of the dining area, and you had to walk a 2x12 plank across deep water to get to it. I've never had balance that was any good, and I didn't want to walk across that plank. I went to the table and told a little white lie. I advised my customers against having the ice cream because it had been melted and frozen over more than a time or two. They thanked me for telling them so. So, I got out of that one. But I didn't see how I could keep getting out of walking the plank, so to speak, so I just told the boss lady I wouldn't be back. I felt good about my decision, besides the 25-mile drive one way just didn't make much sense.

Later on, Wayne and I were presented with the opportunity to run our own bar. You bet we took that chance. It was called Elkhorn Tavern. It was a fun little place on Fourth Street in Coeur d'Alene. I worked days and Wayne worked nights. He also continued to cut hair during the day. One day this gal came into the bar and asked me if I arm-wrestled. I said, "I guess so." We started the match, but neither of us could put the other down. She told me she beat every woman around and she would be back in two weeks and we would do it again. I said OK. We had wooden bar stools which were very heavy. On the weekends, I worked nights and gave Wayne some time off. He tended bar on Sundays during the day, so every night I would clean up the floor. I was the swamper. I picked up the bar stools and put them on the bar so I could mop. They were heavy, but I wanted to build up my arm muscles, just in case a certain challenger to my toughness came back to the bar for a wrestling match. I also continued to work out my muscles when I was at home. I've always been pretty focused when setting goals for myself, and disciplined in trying to meet them. But, damn it—that woman never did show back up. I was disappointed because I was ready to put her down. All that work to build up my arms and no show. But one good thing came out of it all. . . with all that exercise, my bust size went from a 34B to a 36C. I was happy about that.

Zig came up to Coeur d'Alene to see Andrea.

She was still a little thing, not yet in school. He wanted to take her home to Fallon for the summer. I agreed and they were both happy about it. Then my folks came up to visit and wanted to take Tommy, who was now about 12-years-old home for the summer to help on their farm in Fallon. I agreed to that as well. That left Patti, 14, home alone for the summer. She got lonesome and wanted to go to her grandparents, too, so Wayne and I drove her down.

Nevada Calls Me Back

Well Wayne and I weren't back in Coeur d'Alene very long before we got damn lonesome without the kids. And while we were down to Fallon, dropping off Patti, we realized how much we missed Fallon, too. Finally, we decided just to move back there. It was 1966. I went to work for the Lauf Corporation, the company that ran the Nugget casino on the corner of Maine and Williams, as a Keno writer. Wayne went back to working for a barber. We rented a house on Stillwater Avenue. We and the kids were all happy to be home. I worked nights and Wayne was home watching over the kids. It seemed to be working out OK, but then, for some reason, Wayne started to drink heavily, and got to where he didn't do much with or for me, or the kids. Once in awhile, he'd make Swedish pancakes for the kids, but that was about it. No, he spent most of his time guzzling gin-and-tonics while sunbathing with a reflector. Yes, odd! Wayne was always such a great man, but the drinking was getting worse. I tried talking to him, but it was difficult to unsuccessful. We kept on like that for another 12 months or so. In 1968 Wayne was drinking really badly, and he announced to me that he wanted to go back to Coeur d'Alene again. I said I couldn't leave Fallon—not again, not then—so we divorced.

I continued working at the Nugget. I had some good friends who worked there with me, especially my girlfriend Thelma, and a man named Cubby McCain. (Funny, his real name was John McCain—not the senator!) One evening I was going into work and somebody stopped me on the street and asked me if I had heard about Thelma. I asked him what he was talking about? The stranger said Thelma's husband had shot and killed her. He had accused her of seeing another man. Hell, he was seeing another woman—and it wasn't me, by the way! But, he killed her. It was awful. My god, that was a terrible night for me, working and listening to people talk about her. She was a beautiful gal. We were close friends. We were all so sad. I believe her husband died while still in prison.

I made some wonderful, dear friends while working at the Nugget. Two of them were Shirley and Ruth. Around one Christmas in the late 60s, the three of us got laid off temporarily. Given the season, we decided to round up our kids and go to Carol Summit, about 80 miles from Fallon, to get our Christmas trees. Ruth had five kids, and Shirley had four. The permits cost $5 each. We could only afford two. So off we went to Carol Summit. It was snowing as we made our way up to a spot high on the mountain. When we arrived, Shirley and Ruth went up the side of the mountain, while I stayed down to look for pine nuts. I yelled at the gals on the mountain that I had found a pile of pine nuts. They yelled back affirmatively and encouragingly. It was still snowing and raining at the same time. Still, this pile of nuts appeared unusually shiny. I bent over to pick up one and guess what— it was a pile of deer poop! Shirley and Ruth laughed so hard, they darn near fell off the side of the mountain.

Even though we only had two permits, they cut six trees. Ruth and I were wet and cold, so we drank some brandy. Then I suggested we go into Gabbs to get something to eat. Tom had a bar and restaurant there. He liked the unexpected chance to see the kids, and they were excited to see their dad. He treated us to steak, potatoes, and drinks. Shirley didn't drink—not because she was driving, but because she just didn't drink. Tom wouldn't take any money from us. That's a good ex-husband!

Then I further suggested we go to Hawthorne and play a little Keno at the El Capitan, where I knew the owner, Woody. We bellied up to the bar and I had a few more drinks before Shirley and I played a ticket. We played eight numbers in the 50 row. And, lo and behold, it came up for seven, which at that time paid $800! Gosh, we were happy, to say the least. We gave Ruth $100 and split the rest between Shirley and me. We also tipped the Keno people. So we ate again and headed home to Fallon. It was a great night and a good Christmas come early.

There were a lot of us gals working in one of the nine bars on Maine Street in those days. The perfect number, in fact, to make our own ball team. And, that's just what we did. The first game, I was the catcher. Oh my, was that ever a job to get all that gear on. By the time I did, I could hardly get into my squat position. The next game, I told the gals I was going out to right field. We had a blast of a time, and people paid to see us play. We were the Merchanettes, and I'll tell you, just like the movie, we were a league of our own.

Husband Number Four

I kept working at the Nugget, alongside Cubby most of the time, as he was also a Keno writer. We started going to bars together after our shift was over at 2 a.m. We were together pretty steady for about six or eight months, and he wanted to get married, so we did. That was 1969. I was just on the entry side of my 40s. We moved into his house on Stillwater Avenue. My two girls lived with us. Tommy stayed on the ranch with my folks; he loved it out there.

Cubby and I got along for awhile, but when we'd come home after work around 3 a.m., Cubby would sleep until noon while I got the girls off to school, cleaned house, etc. He never did much of anything but smoke and drink coffee. I never smoked; I didn't like it, and really, had a hard time being close to it. In 1972, I quit at the Nugget only because I didn't want to work with Cubby anymore. Overall, it wasn't too good of a marriage, as Cubby drank pretty well, and I did a little of that myself, too. We were married for three years.

A '70s Woman Unto Herself

About the same time Cubby and I divorced, I went to work at the Corral Bar on Center Street (now Jack's Club). Actually, I was more involved in that venture than just working

there. . .I leased the place. I didn't have much money, so the people I leased it from let me stay in their doublewide on Front Street for basically free; I only had to pay a small space rent. I paid them $650 a month for the bar. Tough price, but I knew I could make it. I knew I could be successful. And, I loved that bar. To me, it was just beautiful. I had to sell a lot of booze to stay afloat. But, you know, I wasn't a half-bad businesswoman. And, it was a good little bar.

So, here I was, 44-years-old, going it alone for the first time in a long time, or at least on my own without a man, running my own business. My children were 20, 18 and 12. Patti had started her life's career and passion, working at a veterinarian supply store called Walco's. Tommy was training to become a police officer. Andrea lived over at her dad's house most of the time.

I had a lot of fun in the Corral Bar. We got a lot of construction guys in regularly. They were a great bunch and just made my dayshift for me. I had two gals working for me—one Indian woman, Frances, and one older, large German woman everybody called Butch. Now I can't say one way or the other as to Butch's exact status, given her name. Moreover, I didn't care one way or the other. All I know is she lived with one man for some 50 years. He was in the Navy, and she was quite a bit older than him, or so it seemed. The two of them died one year apart. Frances and Butch both were great gals, honest and good workers.

One day this guy named Aaron came into the bar and had a few drinks. We talked, about nothing. Then he kept coming back. He was about 25-years-old and divorced. (He ended up being the only one of my husbands—out of four Irishmen, one Swede, and one Pollock—who had been married before). I understood that he was just prowling around. And he was definitely good-looking. He offered to buy me a drink. I was tending bar that day, but I had a drink with him. And then I had some more drinks with him. He finally left for the evening. I decided I should be better prepared for the next time he came in, and wanted me to visit and drink with him. I was a brandy-and-water drinker, so I put a brandy bottle full of tea in the well, and a vodka bottle full of water. I instructed the gals, that if he came back, to pour my drink from the imposter bottles. Hey, I didn't want to take the shingle off the roof. I mean, *I* couldn't refuse a drink; it was a ring up on the cash register for me!

About a week went by, and here he comes. Aaron asked if he could buy me a drink. I said yes, and looked at the gals and nodded. They knew what to do. They poured from "my bottle." This went on for awhile and when Aaron excused himself to the men's room, I told Frances to pour me a real brandy as I thought he might be getting suspicious. She poured the brandy over the rocks and set it in front of me. Upon his return, sure enough, Aaron made the underlying comment, "Boy, you really hold your liquor." I agreed with him. He said, "Let me taste your drink." I did, relieved, and silently patting myself on the back for the good move on my part. We sat there and talked for a long time.

As time went on, Aaron kept coming in, and finally, at 20 years my junior, he asked me out. We went out to dinner, and then, we went in. . .to bed. I've always said 25 goes into 45 better than the other way around! Uh-huh, I mean exactly what you're thinking. Well, it's true! Anyhow, we started going out more, and pretty regularly. One afternoon Aaron came in and the bar was full of workers. It was around Thanksgiving. There was a couple drinking down at the end of the bar and they were telling me how they were going to his brother's house for the holiday dinner. I said to the people to tell their brother that I sent my love. I always said that to different people. Well, Aaron, being the hotheaded Irishman he was, got pissed off at my salutations sent to an acquaintance, and he jerked me up from the stool and drug me out to his car. He yelled, "If you want to give him your love then you can!" I yelled back, "For Christ's sake, it's just a figure of speech!" But, crazy, irrational, young Aaron drove like an idiot over to the man's house and told me to get out of the car. I said, "I'm not getting out, you son of a bitch!" So he took me to my house and dropped me off. I was hoping he wouldn't come back, but he did. He apologized to me, but I gave him the cold shoulder for awhile before I went out with him again. I always said about Aaron that he was good in bed but crazy in the head.

I had been in the Corral Bar for about a year when New Year's Eve arrived. I planned a celebration for my customers. I got a turkey and all the trimmings. The bar was full. It was a good night to make money. The music was playing and everyone was having a great time. I was becoming even more excited about one of my New Year's resolutions—that is, to sign a new lease on my bar! And, lo and behold, the restaurant (Long Branch it was called—run by a lady who went by the name of Boots) next door caught on fire! The smoke was just pouring through "the hole in the wall"—aka the window through which my customers could order food while they were drinking. I grabbed the money out of the register, and Aaron helped gather up the turkey and some of the trimmings. We got out most of my liquor inventory, too, thank goodness. Everyone got out safely, so I just invited all the customers over to my mobile home. We put the turkey in the back of Aaron's car. I took the money sack and stuffed it up the turkey's butt—a pretty safe place, I thought. I know—who would have thought of that?—Only me! Off we went to the mobile home and all of us had a great time, squeezed into my home, eating and drinking, visiting and laughing.

The firefighters had come and hosed down the bar to prevent it from burning up completely. There was about a foot of water in there. The next day, the girls, Aaron and I got mops and buckets and swamped the place out. I needed to get that place dry. We turned the heat up on high and that helped a lot.

What a job it was getting that place ready to go. Again, Aaron, the strong Irishman that he was, hauled the humongous register back into the bar all by himself. I got some insurance money and bought more stock. I had tap beer and I kept all the kegs in my walk-in ice box. It was so nice and cool back there; I used to go in there whenever I was having a hot flash. I'd sit on the kegs to cool off and relax. One of those times when I was sitting in there taking a little break, a big guy opened the door and attacked me. I recognized him as a customer who had come in the bar that day, but I didn't know him. I screamed and pushed him up against the wall. Some of the customers in the bar heard me and came to my rescue. Boy, was I happy to see them! They did a good job spooking the guy—he just ran off and never came back.

There was this gal by the name of Vi (pronounced with a long-sounding "i") who made some wonderful, little cakes, on the side. I used to have her make cakes for my customers on their birthdays. I'd also buy them a drink, and all of us in the bar would sing along with "Happy Birthday" on the juke box. I know they really appreciated this gesture from me. And, I in turn, cherished all that they did for me, as customers and neighbors.

I used the cakes to get other messages across, too. There was this one construction guy named JD who came in, regularly, and sometimes, I'll tell you, he just acted like an asshole. So, for his birthday, I had Vi make JD a cake with a hole in the middle of it with chocolate frosting running down from it. I had her write on the cake, "Happy Birthday, Asshole." He didn't like it very well, but his wife did!

Husband Number Five

Around 1975, Aaron and I decided to get married in Reno. What a mistake that was. Live and learn they say. We had a little house on Front Street and lived there for three years.

There came a point though when I started to wonder why he had to go to Lovelock—a little town about an hour east of Fallon—all the time. I went to my psychic and she told me he was messing around with some blond gal.

One day while Aaron was gone, there was a knock on the door. There stood some guy I didn't know with a rifle in his hand. I said, "Come in." He asked me where my husband was. I guessed that he was probably in Lovelock, again. The man—who finally introduced himself as George—declared, "I think my wife is with him." I told him I was sorry for him and his kids, but that if, in fact, his wife was with my husband, then she was just doing me a big favor. He said he was going over to Lovelock to kill the two of them.

When he left, I called one of my gal friends to come over and get me so we could head for Lovelock to see the action. On the way there, we saw a tow truck pulling George's pickup back to Fallon. I said to my girlfriend, "It must have happened." We drove around to all the motels in Lovelock, but we didn't see anything unusual going on. So, we drove back to Fallon, she dropped me off at home, and I went to bed.

The next day—a Sunday morning—I found out that George's son had called the cops on George the night before. Apparently, George had also told his son that he was going to kill the wife and Aaron. The cops picked up George before he made it to Lovelock, and threw him in jail, just overnight and mostly for his own safety. Then, for some reason, the cops ordered Aaron to leave Fallon. That was sure OK by me, but I didn't want to be at the house when Aaron came by to get his things. So I called my friends—Judy and Harold—and asked them to come get me and take me over to the Overland Bar to hide away for awhile. In the meantime, I asked my neighbor to give me a call at the Overland if and when Aaron came home.

When I got to the Overland, I did some drinking, and I took a tranquilizer. Not too much time had passed when the phonecall came. On the other end I heard my neighbor reporting that Aaron was at our house, with a cop escort. Judy and Harold took me back to my house. I went straight past the cop standing in my living room and into the bedroom where Aaron was gathering his clothes. I knocked Aaron down onto the bed and started hitting him in the face. The cop came in and pulled me off of Aaron, but I swirled around, picked that cop up and carried him into the living room. Odd, what a tranquilizer and some booze can do to a person! All kidding aside though, Aaron left for Idaho minutes later and I was glad of it.

The cop went back to the cop shop, and apparently started hootin' and a hollerin' about how I, shall we say, moved him from Point A to Point B. The cop exclaimed, "Honest to God, I have never seen a woman in my life that was as strong as this one! She picked me right up, no problem, and carried me into the living room!" One of the other cops asked, "What was her name?" The first cop answered, "Dolly!" The other cop stated back, matter-of-factly, "She is my mother." The cop and my son had a big laugh that night.

Aaron stayed gone for about two weeks. When he came back to Fallon, briefly, I told him to get the divorce papers started, and that I wanted the house. After the divorce, I heard that he and that gal he was cheating on me with got married and moved to Idaho. I liked that news. I learned later that Tom and his brother who was a cop from New Mexico paid Aaron a visit at some point. Those two big guys put Aaron up against the wall in some alley and made it very clear what might happen to him if he ever touched me again. I liked that news too.

Time For a Change ~ Humor Ever the Same

After about three years of successfully operating the Corral Bar, and loving just about every minute of it, I decided to let go of it. People always asked me if I ever dealt cards, and when they learned no, they've wondered why. I never was a dealer, I think, because my first husband, Tom, was such a gambler, and he lost everything. So I just always stayed away from cards. After the Corral Bar, I was 45-years-old. I'd been there, done that—and then some. I was ready for some kind of change.

But while I waited to see what that change might be exactly, I went to work briefly for Papa Wong at the Sagebrush Club, running Keno. Mr. Wong, (and I think Chinese people in general), was great to work for. They treat you very well. Mr. Wong gave us lunch each shift. Unfortunately, I didn't work for him very long, as he passed away, I think from a reaction to the flu shot.

I had a customer who came in every day to play some Keno, who seemed to always be drunk. I always say, "I moved to Fallon in 1956, and knew every drunk in town for plenty years after!" I told Ruth that I was going to tell this particular customer a big story just to play a joke on him. So, one day, when he was actually half-sober, I said to him, "Bob, do you remember when you and I had a roll in the hay and then took a bath in my pink bathtub with claw feet? We even fooled around in the tub. We had so darn much fun and you told me you loved me." He looked at me and said somewhat confused, "Did it really happen?" I said with a straight face, "Yes, it did." I didn't see him for a couple of weeks. I think he was trying to get his head wrapped around my story, because he was married. I almost died laughing. The next time he came in, he was sober and I confessed to him it was a joke. Oh, he was so relieved, and we laughed about it together.

Some 40 years later, I saw Bob in the hospital. He had long sobered up; he was there getting some kind of help with his breathing. I sat down by him and his fourth wife (not the wife he was married to when I played the joke). She knew the story of the joke I played on Bob decades before. Bob said to me, "I hear you are writing a book." He paused and then added, "Don't put my name in it." I said, "Bob, there are all kinds of Bobs around —Bob Jones, Bob Smith and Bob Up and Kiss my Butt—what difference does it make?" He said, "I guess it doesn't." I hadn't seen him in years. I think he was a very sick man that day, but a tough one, too—bless his heart.

Making people laugh was always been something important to me—for both them and myself. I've never forgotten the time of my first mammogram. Now, I know countless women before me have endured it, as will countless women to come, but still, when the technician put my tit in that machine and was pressing down so damn hard on me, I yelled at her, "What in the hell are you doing!" She said it was the government that wanted me to do this. I yelled, "Piss on the government. If you don't let up on this son of a bitch, I'm coming after you when I get my tit out of this wringer!" I was pissed and she knew it, so she let up on me. I went straight into to my doctor's office, (Dr. Barr was his name), and expressed my shock and anger over what had happened. He just started laughing hysterically and said to me, "Dolly, you are the most wonderful patient I've ever had." Then he asked me to promise if I ever moved away, to still come back and see him. I did a time or two and gave him a big hug and kiss on his cheek. His fondness for me was mutual.

I've kept doing things like that all my life. I always wanted to make people smile and not take things too seriously, and I was successful at that pretty often. One time when seeing a specialist, I had to fill out all those medical forms. On the box that read "Sex," I wrote "Yes." When I got into the doctor's office, he just laughed and said, "That is the first time in my career that anyone has ever said that." He was pleased with me.

I keep them laughing because I think it is, indeed, good medicine, for them and me. I did the same thing when I applied for a job at Ridley's grocery store in Weiser, Idaho. On the application, there was that box again that said, "Sex." So I answered honestly again, "Yes." The man who owned the store called me the next day and said, "Come back down here to the store. I've got to meet you." That afternoon, I went to see him, and he declared, "You're hired." I enjoyed working for him as a checker, but it was only for about three months, because it turned out, I was too damn old for that job. I had applied for it, just for something else to do for fun, but I was close to 70 then, and the ol' girl just wasn't what she used to be, you know what I mean? Hell, picking up a watermelon at that age, for me, was like picking up a train!

When Papa Wong passed away in 1978, he was one of the head guys of the Chinese Mafia—I imagine it was just something he naturally fell into, by way of his family's history, over in California. But I'll tell you, he and his family were the type to really celebrate a life, too. I liked their perspective and style. A few other girlfriends—Ruth, Stella and Dorothy—and I attended his funeral in San Francisco.

Stella drove because she knew the city best out of the four of us. Before we took off, I decided to put some hotdogs under the hood of the car, with onions on them. About halfway to San Francisco, the gals in front said, "We smell onions." Ruth and I were in the back seat drinking brandy and didn't pay much attention to them. But again, they said, "My god, we really smell onions. What is wrong with this car?" I told them to stop so I could check under the hood. I announced playfully, "Lunch is served on the manifold." They were excited because we were hungry. We ate the hot dogs on the side of the road and then continued on our way to San Francisco.

The Wongs had a motel room waiting for us. It didn't cost us a dime. It was really nice of them. We went to the funeral in a theater in China Town. It had a stage and, my gosh, there were so many flowers, it looked like a florist shop. The family was on the stage. I quickly learned that when Chinese women cry at funerals, they really wail. It was the oddest thing we had ever heard.

After the funeral, we followed the procession of cars through China Town, round and round. It seemed like thousands of people were on the sidewalks. We were told to follow the orange Volkswagen to the cemetery. We were talking and for some damn reason that orange car went in between some other cars and we got lost. Driver Stella said, "Well, we'll do the best we can to try and find the darn place." After an hour or so we found the cemetery. We were very late. Then we were told to meet everyone back in China Town at the Dragon Inn restaurant for dinner. That was something else. We sat at a big round table with a Lazy Susan in the middle of the table that was loaded with booze and Chinese food. It was all so good. We ate and drank and then we went to the motel. Everything was free. They even told us to use the telephones to call wherever we wanted to. How fantastic.

After Papa Wong passed away, the Sagebrush sold out to the Lauf Corporation. So, interestingly enough, I found myself back at the Nugget running Keno again. Cubby was long gone from there, so that was a good thing, and I was doing good work like I always had, but I was wanting to get out of the casino business. I'd had my fill of them.

I heard there was some kind of opening at the Churchill County Telephone Company, so I went over there and put my name in. I told them I would gladly take part-time. I went back several times in the next couple of weeks and asked if there were any openings, but the supervisor, named Lois, kept saying no. Finally, I decided to try another strategy. I called the florist and asked her to send three roses to that supervisor, and to write on the card: I still want the job. About three days later the supervisor called me and told me to give my two-weeks notice at the Nugget. Oh, Happy Day for me! For the next four years, I happily worked at the phone company as an operator. I loved that job; Lois, and my other boss, Joe Lister, were both good people to work with.

Husband Number Six ~ Saving the Best for Last

Somewhere in those four years, I decided to take up golf. I asked one of my gal friends— Sharon— if she wanted to go over to the golf course in Fallon—called Desert Aire—with me; I had heard there was a Pro out there who was giving lessons. Sharon was game—no pun intended!—so on my day off, we went out for a lesson. The Pro's name was Preston, and he was also the owner of the course. Turned out, too, that another friend of mine—Dana Buchanan— leased out the bar in the clubhouse, with her husband, Kevin. Sharon and I soon became regulars out at the golf course; we had many beautiful days out there, and plenty of good times. To this day, Sharon and I still keep in touch. She lives in Canada. It's such a blessing to have friends all over the world.

Preston—or as all his friends called him,

Pres—was working on a compressor out at his ranch in Dixie Valley one day, and just wasn't feeling good and right. He went into his house and called a neighbor who lived five miles away. Thank goodness she was home. She took Pres into the hospital in town, and the staff there thought his symptoms deemed best that he go on into Reno to Washoe Medical Center. Then, the staff at Washoe referred him to Sacramento where Pres ended up having his first open heart surgery. His doctor was from India and he told Pres, "After you recover from surgery, do not ever eat or drink anything from a cow again. It plugs up the arteries."

Before Pres got into golf course business, he was already a landowner with his dad and sister. They had two sections of land in Dixie Valley. I remember thinking when Pres shared this with me that that is a lot of land. He owned a bunch of apartments in Long Beach, California, too, with his sister. She lived there and took care of them. Pres and his dad ran the Dixie Valley land for a period of time together until his dad decided to move into an apartment in Fallon. Eventually, he moved into a rest home. When he passed, (he was in his late 90s), he left the land to Pres. Years later though, when Pres got out of the hospital in Sacramento and got home to Fallon, he put the land up for sale and put the money he made into improving the golf course. Occasionally, his sister would come up to Fallon and start throwing orders around to Pres and all the employees at the course. Pres didn't like that too much, so he made a deal with her: she could have the Long Beach apartments all to herself, and in return, release her part in the golf course entirely to him. She agreed.

After a few months of going to the golf course regularly, I asked Dana, "Is that Pro married?" She said no. Good answer, so I asked a follow-up. "Has he ever went out with anyone?" Bob, one of Pres' employees and good friends, who was standing near, answered, "I've known Pres for more than 20 years and he doesn't take women out. And," he added, "he doesn't like boys." I told myself: I like this man. He was such a handsome man, and so kind; everyone loved him. He ended up being the best man I've ever met. Dana, quick to notice my interest, announced that she would set something up. I waited, and one day soon after, she called me and said, "We are going out with a bunch of people, including Pres, so you should come along too."

I told Pres point-blank from the beginning, "I've been married five times and had a love affair with one of your members." He quickly and calmly responded, "If I didn't like you Dolly, I wouldn't be here talking to you." So, that's how we got started.

A short time later, Pres asked me to go with him to Lovelock, of all places. He was going over there to talk to some people who were interested in putting in a golf course. While he met with them, I hung out at Felix's Bar. I knew the owners—Leon and Dee Gurley. Pres, incidentally, wasn't a drinker. Nope, never drank or smoked—pure as the driven snow, that boy. I never smoked—found it disgusting—but yes, I put my share of liquor away, for sure. But, hey, I never got a ticket for anything deviant. I only got one traffic ticket, ever. It was in Weiser, Idaho, when Pres was in the hospital. I was driving along, thinking of him, and went through a school zone at 30 mph. When the cop who pulled me over and asked that weird question they always do, you know—"Do you know why I stopped you, mam?" I answered quietly, blankly, "No." He said the normal fine for my offense was $150. I about fainted. But after he came back from his car, he informed me that he was only going to charge me $53. I had told him I just wasn't paying attention because I was thinking about my husband who was in the hospital in Weiser, so maybe he felt a little human and had a change of heart. Whatever the reason, I'm glad to this day for the lesser charge.

I was comfortable visiting with Dee and Leon until Pres finished up with his business. We drove back to Fallon and Pres took me out to dinner and then dropped me off at home. He never made any advances toward me and that was OK with me. I was confident he liked me, and remembered from Bob's comment that Pres was most definitely not gay!

I kept working at the telephone office as an operator, and seeing Pres a lot. In the meantime, a young couple—Tom and Carrie Wright—rented the downstairs part of the club house and made it into a restaurant called "The Calico Kitchen." It was a darling place that served a sizable and loyal customer base.

We'd been going together for several weeks when Pres came over to my house to see me unexpectedly one evening. He wasn't there very long before he led me into the bedroom. This was Pres's first time with a woman; I could tell he was nervous. But I fixed that. He enjoyed it. And, everytime we were together after that, he'd point to the bedroom, which was very OK with me. It was so peaceful being with him. He was such a good man.

We had been loving one another for about four years when he came to my house and asked me to go get some Chinese dinner with him. We did just that, but oh boy, was the food ever awful. We left that place and were sitting in the car when he revealed to me that he had sold the golf course. Oh, my stomach just dropped. He said he was going to California. I was upset, of course. Then he said, "I wouldn't expect for you to go with me unless we were married." I leaned over, looked at him intently, and said, "My god, I didn't think you were ever going to say those words to me." We'd been going together for four years, and drunk or sober, I had never said anything about marriage. I continued chattering excitedly to him about how I never expected marriage in our relationship, and how, afterall this would be my sixth marriage, and on and on and on. Pres just quietly, but sweetly said to me, "Stop talking." Well, do you think I'd keep my mouth shut for long? As soon as Pres dropped me off at home, I went right down to see Tom and Carrie, and blurted out the wonderful news that Pres had proposed to me. They were so happy. I remember, even though it was my sixth time around, Dana threw me a lovely bridal shower. She lives in Pittsburgh these days, but we keep in touch, and she is as dear a friend as ever.

On February 3, 1980, we did it. About three months after Pres proposed, he and I were married on Dana and Ron's ranch out in Stillwater. It was a fantastic ceremony and celebration with about 50 friends and loved ones. It was an absolutely wonderful day.

Pres was a pilot in the military. I've never forgotten how he looked in his uniform in some pictures I once saw. What a handsome man he was. I looked at him on our wedding day much like I remember looking at those pictures. Oh, how I was in love with him. I had loved all of my other husbands, but I was *In Love* with Pres. There is a big difference. Pres was a jewel of a man. He was very naturally, kind-hearted. At age 51, (and Pres at 63), I'd found *the* love of my life. Indeed, my soul mate.

Me and my beloved Preston Kyle – 1980

Pres' sister had offered to give us a trip to Hawaii for our honeymoon, but he was still mad at her for the way she acted at the golf course years before, so we didn't accept her gift. Still, we moved to California—Long Beach, in fact—and lived just a few miles from his sister. So, obviously, I quit my job at the telephone company—the best job I ever had. I worked there for four years and if Pres hadn't asked me to marry him, I'd stayed at the job for as long as I could have. It was a great place to work, with great people. Joe had told me, "If this marriage doesn't work out, Dolly, you always have a job here." That was so sweet of him to say.

In California, Pres and I rented a nice condo, and soon became close friends with our landlords, Al and Mona Lewis. Pres got a job in the Pro shop at Los Alamitos Golf Course, and I worked at the snack bar way out in the middle of the course with a gal named Jeanie. What a sweetheart she was. We became part of that golf community so quickly because Bob had moved down there some time before and was the Pro at Los Alamitos. We loved working and living there. Pres had business cards that listed him as the Pro. I made up a fun business card for him and me, as a couple. It read: Pres and Dolly Kyle, The Pro and the "Pro"fanity! Hey, if the shoe fits! Our personalities definitely complimented one another. Oh, Pres and I always had a good time, and loved each other so. We were married for 24 wonderful years. He was a neat man. All the doctors in Weiser and Fallon would tell you that. He taught most of them golf! Pres was a sweetheart.

As much as we loved our life in Los Alamitos, fate or something, returned us, four years later, to Fallon. The daughter of the man to whom Pres sold the golf course in Fallon was in a terrible accident, so the man, devastated, just walked away from the course. So we went back to resume care and management of the course—which was in terrible shape.

We hated to leave California. Darn it. Tommy came down to help us load our belongings onto a U-Haul. He drove the truck, Pres drove our station wagon, and I drove another car we had just bought. We had quite a caravan going. Even though I was going to miss Long Beach, I sure as hell was not going to miss the traffic; the freeways in California are so crowded with people, and that was back in the early 80s! For that, I was damn glad to get back to Nevada. I didn't think we had too many crazy people there. . .well, at least not as many as California! I'd always thought of Fallon as a nice, quiet town.

We lived in the apartment at the golf course, and worked hard. We'd get up at 5 a.m. to start getting things ready for the golfers each day—everything from making coffee to maintaining the health and appearance of the course. We had such good members; they are who kept the course alive since before Pres came into the picture the first time.

In the late 80s, the man who had been purchasing the course decided he wanted it back, so we headed to court to settle that dilemma. The judge ordered that he had to come up with the down payment and back taxes, immediately, which he did, so, suddenly, Pres and I found ourselves without a home. But we were thrilled at the opportunity for a new adventure! We moved to Twin Falls, Idaho—a beautiful place—where Pres had some family and friends. We bought a duplex, and rented out one side. We loved it!

In the winters, we'd go to Palm Springs. Oh, what a great time we had! Pres was tickled to play on a new course there—the La Quinta. He made the course's first hole-in-one. I was as excited as he was about that. I understand the little plaque with Pres' name on it is still on the top of the wall at La Quinta in Palm Springs. In his lifetime, Pres made six holes-in-one.

Our second winter in Idaho, we retreated to Phoenix to a place called Happy Trails. We knew a lot of people there already because most of the golfers from Fallon had purchased winter homes there. It was a great place where we had nothing but fun times with good friends. That is, until Pres got really sick. He spent four months in the hospital recovering from a heart attack. I stayed the nights in our motorhome at Happy Trails. But I'll tell you, I was glad to go to the hospital every day, where it was air-conditioned and cool. It got so damn hot there in Phoenix. It was up to 127 degrees! Wow, it was hot!

Just before Pres had his heart attack, we had bought a lot in a beautiful subdivision near, but outside of Happy Trails. We had gotten as far as making a down payment and picking out the house model that we wanted built. While Pres was sick in the hospital, I called the salesman and told him we weren't going to be able to live there. When Pres had been in the hospital for two months, the salesman came to me and said, "The house is built. Pres has to sign these papers so you can move in." I told him we were not moving because Pres wasn't expected to live and I was not going to sign anything.

I decided at that time to go to Happy Trails and pick out a lot and put a doublewide on it. I went down to the sales offices, just like I knew what I was doing. We got it all set up, so everything would be ready for Pres whenever the doctors released him. Strange what people will do on the outside to compensate for what they are feeling, or fearing, on the inside. In the back of my mind, I knew there was a chance that the doctors wouldn't release Pres, but because I just couldn't allow myself to even imagine that, I kept myself busy preparing for his homecoming. I had stairs built up to the doublewide front door so Pres wouldn't have to step too high. I didn't say a word to Pres about all this because he was so darn sick; I didn't want him to have anything to worry about. I'd never done anything like that before—meaning, making such a big purchase and arrangements all on my own, and certainly not without my partner, Pres. That is what's interesting about love, I think. Real, true, deep love. If it's for the one we love, or because of the indescribable love we have for them, we can do things we never dreamed. Two months after that, when Pres was ready to get out of the hospital—well, I told him about what went down with the other house, and then about the doublewide. I told him everything, and he agreed with me. He said, "I know you loved the idea of the new house, but you were happier in Happy Trails, and I was too." How wonderful is that? This was one of a few personal experiences in my life that showed me the meaning and joy of being one with someone.

We met so many wonderful people at Happy Trails. What a nice place it was to be, year-round, even with the blistering heat in the summer. We sold the duplex in Idaho, and moved out of the motorhome and into the doublewide. We hired a mover to bring our furniture, but all of our neighbors at Happy Trails helped us get moved in. What a bunch of great people in those parks!

Pres was getting better and stronger by the day, but his golf game wasn't going well. He couldn't do what he wanted to do as a golf pro anymore, or even just as a guy who loved to play the game. So he decided that we should sell the doublewide and get a 5th wheel and a truck to pull it and go somewhere else. Friends of ours had told Pres that land was cheap in Weiser, Idaho, so we drove up there one day, just to check it out. We stayed in a motel for about a week looking around for a ranch. We found a nice one about seven miles from town, but I told Pres that after going through him being so ill for so long in Arizona, I wanted to live closer to a hospital from now on.

We found a beautiful plot of 90 acres. It didn't have a house, just a pump house and big machine shop, and an open hay barn and corrals. And, there were three wheel lines on the property. No equipment went with it. It was really nice. The owner had kept it up. There were four girls in his family and they all worked the ranch. He was asking $250,000. That is a lot of money then and now, but Pres wanted it and I figured, after being so darn sick, if he wanted it, let him go for it. Besides, we had the money from the sale of the golf course in Fallon. Anyway, almost suddenly it seemed, we found we had become a couple of Idaho ranch owners!

We temporarily set the 5th wheel up near the pump house which had electricity. We were fine and comfortable but didn't waste any time seeking out something new and larger for our permanent home. We found a beautiful new doublewide—a modular, as the sales guy called it. A contractor put it on a freshly-poured foundation, dug a septic tank for us, and wired the electric. It took some time to do all of this, and it started to get cold while we were still in the 5th wheel. Oh my, was it ever cold up in that country.

In the meantime, we called the same mover who moved us into our Happy Trails home in Arizona to get our furniture out of storage, again, and bring it to Idaho. Our new home was all electric, with three bedrooms and three baths— a really nice place. We moved in on December

3, 1994. I was so happy to get into a house. We put the 5th wheel in the machine shop to protect it from the weather, and later sold it, along with the pick-up. Our new neighbors came over and helped us settle in. Just like our neighbors in Arizona, people were very nice in Weiser.

We had a long winter that year and couldn't do anything until spring. As soon as some warm weather arrived, we got out of the house and started to do some clean up.

There was a nice golf course there in Weiser, which made Pres happy. It wasn't long before he was splitting his days quite satisfactorily between the Weiser Golf Course and the ranch. Pres had made a deal with the former owner, David, who still wanted to be involved with the working of the land. David was a good soul and still handled the bulk of the hay work. Pres was so pleased with this business relationship, and friendship.

We did the irrigating. What a damn job that was with those big wheel lines. We did the gopher thing for awhile, but then had some men come out from town to poison the gophers. David did the hay for three years; after that, Tommy and his wife moved up from Fallon and did all the custom haying for us. Myrna, my daughter-in-law, worked like a horse on that place.

We joked and called them our Hey Farmers, because we said, "Hey, come over here, and help us out!" They put in a big garden and she canned a lot, plus took care of their two little sons. It was great having them there.

Tom already had the equipment to do the haying, so things went along O.K.—that is, until 2000, when Pres got sick again and was in and out of the Weiser hospital. I knew I had almost lost him in Arizona, but this time 'round was horrible for me. I was so afraid that he would die. Then, he just got well. And, he started playing golf again, a lot of the time with the doctors who had been taking care of him. Pres was so happy; I understood that being able to work really hard at that game of golf meant so much more to him than the simple, mindless pursuit it might have appeared to be to anyone else.

We continued doing some of the irrigating, but Tom and Myrna eventually took it over, and that was a relief. We all lived there on the ranch. The boys went to school, and when they came home they had chores to do. They also raised a calf or two.

One year on the ranch, Tommy and Myrna found a deer out in the hills. The little thing had thorny vines all over him. They waited for hours for the mother to come for him, but when it started getting dark, they figured the mother was not likely coming back and decided to bring him home to the ranch. They named him Jasper Jones.

He was just a baby, so they fed him with a bottle filled with goat's milk. He was so darling. He had those cute, little white spots all over him. Tom trained him to use the cat box and by golly, he did.

Time went by and Jasper grew healthy and strong. Tom sent for a permit to keep him, from the Fish and Game department, but they didn't want to issue Tom a permit for some reason or another. So, Tom, quite in love with Jasper by this point, got in touch with an Idaho Senator who was in Boise and told him what the Fish and Game had said. The Senator, somehow, persuaded the Fish and Game to just leave Tom and Jasper well enough alone, just as they were.

Jasper happily roamed the ranch. At night sometimes, Tom would put him in a large pen, but overall, we couldn't fence him in—it was the law of the land, as long as we did not have an official permit for him, but also, in our hearts we wanted him to be free. We wanted him to be safe though, too, so we did get him a red collar with his name and address and our phone number on it. He knew his name. He'd be out in the alfalfa field eating, and I would call, "Jasper, come and see Gramma." He'd turn and come a-leaping back to the ranch house. I'd give him a banana. He loved bananas. He loved my tulips, too. I tried buying some supposed "deer-resistant" plants one time. . .guess what? Jasper ate them anyway. Hell, he didn't know he was a deer. His favorite breakfast was oats and raisins out of Tom's hand in the mornings.

One early Friday morning in 2003, Tom let Jasper out of the pen and then went back in the house. Some dogs scared Jasper and he ran down the road and got out on the highway, heading for Payette, about five miles away. He went into a lady's yard. She saw that he had a collar on, but she was afraid to get close. She called the sheriff's office and they came and picked him up and put him away somewhere.

Tom was out all day, desperately calling and searching for Jasper. Eventually, we got a phonecall from the local Fish and Game office. They had Jasper and said they were going to put him down. Tom told them, "That's what you think!" Tom called the head Fish and Game office in Boise and talked to the big shot. In the meantime,

Tom and Myrna made up flyers and put them all over town, in the grocery stores, gas stations and tire shops. The flyer explained how Jasper had been caught by the Fish and Game and that they were going to put him down. They petitioned people to sign the flyer to get Jasper back safe and sound. Jasper was well-known and well-loved in Weiser. Tom and Myrna used to take him to the schools so the kids could pet him. They collected at least a thousand signatures on the flyers.

On Monday, the Fish and Game called Tom to "come and get his animal." When Tom and Myrna picked up Jasper, he was very thin. They hadn't fed him; those men were bastards. Jasper was so happy to see Tom and Myrna.

The town paper had a big write-up about Jasper. He was quite the celebrity. The schoolchildren and people who knew Jasper all came out to the ranch to see him. Even some of our neighbors were happy Jasper was home, even though he'd eaten up some of their gardens in the past. We could tell Jasper was very happy, too.

Tom called the Fish and Game in Boise and told them that he was sending in money to get a permit for Jasper. It took them six months to get it to him. For some ridiculous reason, they stayed pissed. I guess they didn't have anything else to do! Later on, we would see the Fish and Game on the hill behind our ranch spying on Jasper with binoculars. One time Tom took his binoculars and looked right back at them, straight in their eyes. That was great. What a bunch of jackasses.

We lost Jasper four years later. He had eaten some moldy grain, and it got stuck in his bowels. Tom and Myrna took him to the vet, but the doctor said there was nothing he could do for our dear deer friend. I was visiting in Fallon when all this happened. Tom called, crying on the phone. The whole town was upset.

My heart, too, was deeply broken when we lost Jasper. I was his Gramma. Or at least, he was like a grandkid to me. We had quite the relationship. He brought me joy. I loved him. Having Jasper in my life, I've always believed, was an experience that was just another tribute to my Grandmother, who was so precious to me, and to her wisdom. Living life with Jasper was another chance for me to live life to the fullest.

One day, a lady who knew of our losing Jasper, brought a baby deer to Tom. He and Myrna named her Jasmine, after Jasper. And, another couple brought them a second baby deer that Tom and Myrna named Tammy. Tom trained them both, just as he did Jasper. They stayed in a large fenced-in area, and, used a cat box.

At one point, Tom had a third baby deer named Tia, but one day when she got a little older, a bunch of bucks came through the ranch, and she ran off with one. Sometime later, we discovered she couldn't give up the tame life and had taken up residence on a ranch about 30 miles away. Tom got regular reports on her; she gave birth to a set of twins more than once.

In 2004 Pres got really sick again. This time it was particularly bad. Ironically, on the designated day of love, February 14th —and 11 days after our 24th wedding anniversary—I lost the love of my life—my Pres passed on to God. It was awful for me. I waited a year before I did anything. But then, it was apparent I could not afford to stay where I was anymore, without Pres, but even more, I didn't want to be there anymore, not without Pres. So, I had a big sale of every "thing" I loved, including all my beautiful furniture, and sold the house to Tom and Myrna. I wanted to go back to Fallon where I had a lot of friends, and Patti was still living in Fallon at the time, too.

Going Home

In mid-2005, I got a U-Haul and two friends—Dan Whooley, and also Judy Emerson— came up from Fallon to help me drive back. Dan drove the U-Haul, towing his car behind, and Judy drove my car. I just rode along. My apartment, on Auction Road, wasn't going to be ready until the first of September, so I stayed for a long time at several different friends' places. First, I stayed with Gail Lussier for about six weeks. Then I went over to Judy's, for just about a week because she about froze me to death with her raging air-conditioner. Then I stayed with Betty and Charlie Shetter for about a month. They were very nice and patient. It was tough, especially at my age, to live out of a suitcase, staying with different people, for three months. It wasn't fun. Finally, I got into my apartment in September 2005; I was so happy to get into my own place.

Prior to Pres' passing, I had called the Hospice in Weiser and asked them for their help during his last days. I had talked to the man who ran the Hospice—Dwight—and told him that Fallon needed a Hospice. I don't know if I was clairvoyantly foreboding my last days, certain to come someday, and planting a seed for care that I might need at that time, but by the time I moved back to Fallon, I had all but forgotten about that conversation. A few years later, I heard that a Hospice had been founded in Fallon, so I went down to their offices to visit. I walked in and announced, "I'm Dolly Kyle." Curiously, all the office workers and nurses were particularly happy to see me. They came over to me and exclaimed, "You are the reason we have a job!" I was touched that Dwight had listened to me in Weiser, as I love Fallon so much.

My first ex-husband, Tom, died a month and four days after Pres, on March 18, 2004, in Weiser. Tom had come up to live in Weiser a couple of years before; we had all remained friends over the years. So, when I returned to Fallon, I carried with me, both Tom's and Pres' ashes. Ironic, I know. But sweetly poetic, too. I spread Pres' ashes at the golf course—where we had met, and courted, worked and played, laughed and loved together—and every time I go out there now, I say a prayer for him. I didn't have services for Pres, at his request. My son and daughter's dad was interned in Fernley at the Vet's cemetery. We held a funeral for Tom, and I had a hard time with it. He was my first husband, and Pres my last. They are both at peace now.

I certainly have led an exciting, blessed life. I'm definitely grateful. I've done so many fun and outrageous things, my resume' would be a pretty colorful one, indeed. Thinking how such a document would be pretty funny, and entertaining, I designed my own business card. . . well, it's actually a personal, NON-business card. And, deliberately so! That's the novelty of it, I suppose. Jasper's place and influence on my life is prominent on the card. The middle of the card reads:

NON BUSINESS CARD
Dolly Kyle
Jasper Jones' Grandmother

Then, all around the edges of the card, it lists my other "jobs, skills and qualifications!" It reads: Things I have done through my life—Bull ride; Clown; Santa; Waitress; Cook; Butcher; Broke Horses; Oh Yes, I also was a Witch, every chance I got turned into a "Motel"; Telephone Operator; Change Girl; Bartender; Secretary; Scuba Diver; Keno Dealer; Office Worker; Pro Shop Owner; Bar Owner; "Hey" Farmer; Deputized as a Deputy for a day; Drove Wild Horses; Drove Cattle; Had a Wonderful Love Life, Boy Did I!

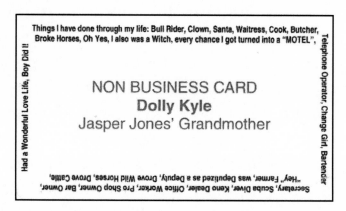

At any rate, I think my Grandmother would've been pleased for the most part with how I've lived my life—definitely according to her wise words: make it a good one, because

You Can't Come Back for Seconds!

CPSIA information can be obtained at www.ICGtesting.com
Printed in the USA
BVOW070642200612

293191BV00003B/278/P